HEBREWS

H. A. IRONSIDE

HEBREWS

An Ironside Expository Commentary

H. A. Ironside

KREGEL
MINISTRY

Hebrews: An Ironside Expository Commentary

Originally published in 1932. Reprinted by Kregel Ministry, an imprint of Kregel Publications, 2450 Oak Industrial Dr. NE, Grand Rapids, MI 49505.

Unless otherwise noted, Scripture quotations are from the King James Version of the Holy Bible.

Scripture quotations marked DARBY are from the Darby Translation.

ISBN 978-0-8254-4660-3

Printed in the United States of America

1 2 3 4 5 / 26 25 24 23 22 21 20

Contents

Preface

These studies appeared serially in the monthly expository magazine *Revelation* during 1931 and 1932, and are now reproduced in book form by kind permission from the original publishers. In preparing for their republication all the papers have been carefully edited and occasionally revised for the sake of greater clearness, though they are substantially unchanged.

—H. A. Ironside

INTRODUCTION

Authorship, Scope, and Outline of the Epistle

Authorship

Who wrote Hebrews? Is it for us to be certain in regard to its human author, and is it of any importance that we should know, since the letter comes to us anonymously? If God meant us to know the author's name would He not have told us? These are questions properly raised, and I desire to try to answer them in all fairness.

I write for those who believe in the inspiration of this epistle, as of all Scripture, and by that term I mean all that was accepted as Scripture in our Lord's day, that is, the entire Old Testament; and also the books regarded as canonical by the Christians of the first century.

Hebrews belongs to this latter collection. This is evidently an integral part of the Word of God. Cut from our Bibles, it would leave a great gap that nothing else could fill. In its own place, it fills that gap admirably and forms in a most marvelous way the connecting link between the economy of the Old and the New Testaments.

It is accredited to Paul the apostle in our English Bibles, as also in many manuscripts, yet from the latter part of the second century there have not been wanting those who have denied its Pauline authorship. It has been variously, ascribed to Apollos, Barnabas, and even to Priscilla, the wife of Aquila! It is strange, if Apollos were the author, that the Alexandrian church never seems to have heard of it, and yet Apollos was of Alexandria. Were he the author, how natural that this church should have had a holy pride in the recognition of his work, and never have permitted his name to be forgotten as the chosen instrument. So far as Barnabas is concerned, there is not a scintilla of evidence that he was its author. If it should be proved that Barnabas were the author of the properly spurious epistle ascribed to him, the difference in style between it and the epistle to the Hebrews is too marked to admit of the thought that both could have been written by the same person. As to Priscilla's authorship, in spite of "certain dainty feminine touches" which a lady expositor thinks she has seen in it, the supposition may be rejected as utterly absurd, and without any foundation in fact.

But does it really make any difference as to who the human author was? I think it does, at least in our understanding of its scope and timeliness. As I have before pointed out, this letter is the last of a series of three epistles forming together a divinely inspired commentary on one Old Testament text, namely Habakkuk 2:4, "The just shall live by . . . faith."[1] Romans expounds the first two words and shows who alone are "the just" before God. Galatians continues the wondrous story and explains how the just "shall live." Having begun in the Spirit they are not to be made perfect by the flesh, but they live by the same faith that justifies. Now Hebrews completes the story, expounding the last two words, showing that it is "by faith" God's pilgrim people walk through this world to His praise and glory. Is it likely that He who is a God of order chose Paul to write Romans and Galatians, but selected some unknown writer to give us Hebrews? Is it not very much more probable that the same servant wrote all three epistles?

Now our second question: May we be certain as to its human authorship, or is it merely a matter of intellectual speculation at best? I believe God has given us definite information on this point: First, we have the well-known statement of the apostle Peter, which would seem conclusive as to the Pauline authorship. "And account that the longsuffering of our Lord is salvation; even as our beloved brother Paul also according to the wisdom given unto him hath written unto you; as also in all his epistles, speaking in them of these things; in which are some things hard to be understood, which they that are unlearned and unstable wrest, as they do also the other scriptures, unto their own destruction" (2 Peter 3:15–16). It should be noted that the apostle Peter writes to the Jewish believers scattered abroad, as his first epistle makes evident. Therefore, of course, he writes to Hebrews. His second epistle was written to the same people. "This second epistle, beloved, I now write unto you; in both which I stir up your pure minds by way of remembrance" (2 Peter 3:1). He declares that "our beloved brother Paul" had written an epistle unto them. Now if he is not referring to this letter to the Hebrews, then there is no such letter preserved, because all Paul's other epistles, written to companies of saints, were addressed to churches of the Gentiles. Then again in this Hebrew letter to which Peter refers, Paul has written "some things hard to be understood, which they that are unlearned and unstable wrest to their own destruction." How true is this of the epistle to the Hebrews! How many thousands of unstable souls have been thrown into greatest agony of mind and perturbation of spirit because of misunderstandings and utterly false interpretations of parts of chapters six and ten. It would seem that Peter could not have indicated more definitely than he has done that he referred to this letter.

Further, in the epistle to the Thessalonians we read, "The salutation of Paul with mine own hand, which is the token in every epistle; so I write. The grace of our Lord Jesus Christ be with you all" (2 Thess. 3:17–18). Here the apostle Paul tells us of the secret mark, if we may so say, placed at the end of every one of his letters, thus guarding saints from deception by forgery. Remember the warning in 2 Thessalonians 2:2, "That ye be not soon shaken in mind, or be troubled, neither by spirit, nor by word, *nor by letter as from us*, as that the day of Christ is at hand." What is this secret mark? It is a message that characterizes his entire ministry, a salutation that emphasizes the *grace* of our Lord Jesus Christ. Let us notice how this secret mark is found at the close of all his genuine letters.

> The grace of our Lord Jesus Christ be with you all. Amen. (Rom. 16:24; observe vv. 25–27 are in the nature of a postscript. The epistle properly ends with v. 24.)
>
> The grace of our Lord Jesus Christ be with you. My love be with you all in Christ Jesus. Amen. (1 Cor. 16:23–24)
>
> The grace of our Lord Jesus Christ, and the love of God, and the communion of the Holy Ghost, be with you all. Amen. (2 Cor. 13:14)
>
> Brethren, the grace of our Lord Jesus Christ be with your spirit. Amen. (Gal. 6:18)
>
> Grace be with all them that love our Lord Jesus Christ in sincerity. Amen. (Eph. 6:24)
>
> The grace of our Lord Jesus Christ be with you all. Amen. (Phil. 4:23)
>
> The salutation by the hand of me Paul. Remember my bonds. Grace be with you. Amen. (Col. 4:18)

> The grace of our Lord Jesus Christ be with you. Amen. (1 Thess. 5:28)

> The grace of our Lord Jesus Christ be with you all. Amen. (2 Thess. 3:18)

> Grace be with thee. Amen. (1 Tim. 6:21)

> The Lord Jesus Christ be with thy spirit. Grace be with you. Amen. (2 Tim. 4:22)

> All that are with me salute thee. Greet them that love us in the faith. Grace be with you all. Amen. (Titus 3:15)

> The grace of our Lord Jesus Christ be with your spirit. Amen. (Philem. 25)

> Grace be with you all. Amen. (Heb. 13:25)

Can there be any question but that here we have Paul's authentication of this letter as written by himself? The proof becomes stronger when we turn to the general epistles, and notice how different are all the endings. Never once is the word grace used excepting in 2 Peter 3:18. There it is "grow in grace," which is, of course, experience, and not the grace that saves. The book of Revelation which is of an altogether different character does use the grace salutation which is quite in keeping with the closing of the New Testament, and we need to remember that it is not an epistle, but a great prophetic treatise.

But why then is the epistle to the Hebrews given anonymously? For this, I think there is a very clear answer. Paul is here writing to his own brethren after the flesh. They were greatly prejudiced against him and his ministry, though he yearned after them with all the fervor of a devoted brotherly love. Yet many of them repudiated his apostleship and feared his attitude toward their ancient ritual. He had tried to overcome this opposition. Upon the occasion of his last visit to Jerusalem, he went so far, in accordance with the suggestion of James, as to pay for the sacrificial offerings of certain brethren about to be released from Nazarite vows. But God would not permit this, for it would have been a virtual denial of the sufficiency of the one offering of the Lord Jesus Christ upon the cross, and so the divinely permitted insurrection against Paul saved him from this apparent inconsistency. Probably during the time of his release, after his first imprisonment and before his second arrest (cf. Heb. 13:23), he was chosen of God to write this letter calling upon believers in the Lord Jesus to separate completely from Judaism, as the entire system was about to be definitely rejected with the destruction of the Jewish temple so soon to take place. Paul therefore acts in accordance with the principle laid down elsewhere, "Unto the Jews I became a Jew that I might gain the Jews" (1 Cor. 9:20). And so he hides his identity for the time being and does not insist upon his own apostolic authority, but rather makes his appeal to the Old Testament Scripture, in the light, of course, of the new revelation.

Scope

Hebrews, then, is the New Testament Leviticus. What Augustine thought of the two Testaments may be very properly limited to these two books. Hebrews is in Leviticus concealed; Leviticus by Hebrews is revealed. This New Testament letter opens up in a marvelous way the typical teaching of the third book of the Law. As that book was given to the people of Israel while still in the wilderness, so this is a letter for wilderness saints; for believers who have left this Egypt world behind, and are a pilgrim host journeying on to the rest that remains to the people of God. It is the "Pilgrim's Progress" from the cross to the coming glory, and therefore it is a call to separation. These believers are called upon to leave:

1. The shadows for the substance.

2. The types for the antitypes. (Or rather, the antitype for the reality, for in this Epistle what we generally call the types are actually designated antitypes, and their fulfillment becomes a reality.)

3. The good things of Judaism for the "better" things of Christianity.

4. The incompleteness of the old dispensation for the perfection of the new.

5. The carnal ordinances serving a temporary purpose for the eternal spiritual verities of the fuller revelation.

6. The earthly sanctuary and all its passing ceremonies for the heavenly sanctuary and its abiding realities.

7. The conditional promises of the old covenant for the unconditional promises of the new. (For although the new covenant has not yet actually been made with Israel and Judah, believers now come under its spiritual blessings.)

In a manner that grips the heart and stirs the mind to its deepest depths, this epistle points out Christ's glories as Son of God and Son of Man. It brings before us, in the fullest possible way, His marvelous person as the Apostle and High Priest of our confession. It presents Him as the One who is far superior to angels through whom the law was given; to prophets through whom God gave partial revelations of His mind; to Moses, the apostle of the old dispensation; to Aaron and his successors, the high priests of the earthly sanctuary; and to Joshua who led them into their temporal inheritance. All these are superseded and surpassed by our Lord

Jesus Christ. Then His work is shown to be the fulfillment of all the former shadows. This work comes before us as partially executed on earth, and now going on in heaven. His sacrifice upon the cross is absolutely perfect and cancels every other, having settled forever the sin question. His intercession in the heavens above sustains His people through all their wilderness journey, and will be carried on continuously until He comes again.

Although written particularly for the enlightenment of believers who had come out of Judaism, it is, of course, for all Christians to the end of the dispensation, for in Christ Jesus there is neither Jew nor Greek. What is true for one is now true for all. How sad to undervalue so precious a portion of the Word (as some, alas, do, who should know better), on the plea that it is "Jewish," and does not give the full Christian position; whereas, the fact of the matter is, it was written to deliver Christians from being Jewish, and to bring them into the full light of the glory shining through the rent veil.

In this dispensation of the grace of God, when "in Christ Jesus there is neither Greek nor Jew," it ought to be evident that all the New Testament Epistles are for all the church of God, to whomsoever they may have been first addressed. This does not make it necessary to overlook the fact that there may be in some of them special applications to local conditions now passed away. But all are for the guidance and instruction of those who belong to Christ and are waiting for His return from heaven.

Outline of the Epistle

In studying any book of the Bible, it is most important to have a clear outline in mind. In this, as in doctrinal matters, we may well give heed to the apostle's admonition in 2 Timothy 1:13, "Hold fast the form of sound words," or, as it has been otherwise translated, "having an outline of sound words." This will save from many incongruous interpretations and applications. He who selects a text at random from a given book with little or no regard to the context, failing utterly to grasp the theme and its unfolding, is almost certain to be misled and to mislead his ignorant hearers, at the same time arousing the pity or contempt of those better instructed. For our present study, I submit the following outline. We have already seen that the theme is the superiority of the New Testament realities to the types and shadows of the former dispensation. In unfolding this theme we find that the Spirit of God apparently divides the epistle into five parts. These may be displayed as follows:

Chapter 1: The Glories of the Son of God (Heb. 1:1–2:4)

- A. God speaking in the Son (Heb. 1:1–4)
- B. The Son greater than the angels (Heb. 1:5–14)
- C. The importance of receiving and holding fast the truth as to the person of the Son (Heb. 2:1–4)

Chapter 2: The Glories and Humiliation of the Son of Man (Heb. 2:5–4:13)

- A. The glory of the Son of Man and His authority (2:5–9)
- B. The perfecting of the Captain of our salvation through suffering (2:10–18)
- C. The glory of the Son over the house of God (3:1–6)
- D. The perfected Savior leading His people through the wilderness to the eternal Sabbath of God: Warning as to coming short (3:7–4:13)

Chapter 3: The Priesthood of the Heavenly Sanctuary Superior to That of Aaron (Heb. 4:14–10:39)

- A. The enthroned Priest after the order of Melchisedek, though of the pattern of Aaron (4:14–7:28)
  1. The man in the glory, our Great High Priest (4:14–5:10)
  2. Warning against apostasy: Safety only in resting upon the Word of God (5:11–6:20)
  3. The Melchisedek priesthood superior to that of Aaron (chap. 7)

- B. The Mediator of the new covenant (chap. 8)
  1. The ascended Priest (8:1–6)
  2. The better covenant supersedes the old (8:7–13)
- C. The perfection of Christ's work (chaps. 9–10)
  1. The earthly sanctuary a shadow of the heavenly (9:1–10)
  2. The superiority of the sacrifice of Christ to all those offered under the old dispensation (9:11–23)
  3. The way into the holiest through the blood of Jesus: His entrance the pledge of ours (9:24–10:22)
  4. Warning against apostasy: Evidences of reality (10:23–39)

Chapter 4: The Path of Faith and the Heroes of Faith in All Dispensations (Heb. 11)

- A. The nature of faith (11:1–3)
- B. Faith exemplified in Antediluvian times (11:4–7)
- C. Faith in view of the promised Seed (11:8–16)
- D. Faith exemplified in the patriarchs from Abraham to Joseph (11:17–22)
- E. Varied experiences of faith from Moses to the later prophets (11:23–40)

Chapter 5: Life in Accordance with the Truth of the New Dispensation (Heb. 12–13)

- A. Warning and encouragement to go on (12:1–17)
- B. Vivid contrasts of the two dispensations (12:18–24)
- C. Intensive warning lest the present truth be refused (12:25–29)
- D. Sundry exhortations (13:1–6)
- E. The call to absolute separation from the old system—Judaism (13:7–21)
- F. Concluding salutations: Paul's secret mark (13:22–25)[2]

According to this, then, in the first division the great truth that is emphasized is that the One in whom God has now spoken is infinitely superior to all the prophets whose writings compose the Old Testament, though it is the same God who speaks in both. But He speaks in fullness in His Son, which was impossible through merely human instruments. The Son is also seen as superior to all angels, for however great their power and might, they are still creatures, but He is the Creator of all things. Throughout this division He is viewed as the Son who has come into the world as Man, but who is nevertheless truly God. For it was not until He became incarnate that God could be said to have spoken in Him. He was the Word from all Eternity, but the Word was uttered in Time when He came into the world as the virgin-born Son of God. It is of all importance to believe and to hold fast the revelation that has been given concerning His glorious person.

In the second division it is rather the Manhood of Christ that is in view. He who is God has become Man, and as Man He is the prototype of what all men should be and of what all shall yet be who are saved through Him. He became Man in order that He might tread the path of faith before us, entering sinlessly into all human experiences, in which He ever sought the glory of the Father. But this alone would not have fitted Him to be the Captain of our salvation. As such, He must be perfected through the suffering of the cross. Ever perfect in Himself as to His character, He nevertheless had to go through the process of perfecting as Savior. In other words, He could not have delivered us from the judgment due to our sins without bearing that judgment Himself. In this division, He is seen to be vastly superior to Moses, the great apostle of the Old Dispensation, and to Aaron, its high priest. Moreover, it is evident that the house built by Moses, the tabernacle in the wilderness in which Moses himself was but a servant, was designed of God to picture both the universe and the people of God as the habitation of the Spirit, over which the Man Christ Jesus, now glorified, is set in authority as Son.

Though now forever beyond the reach of pain and suffering, His tenderness and sympathy are with all His people in the trials they are called upon to endure, and as the Good Shepherd He leads them on through the wilderness to the rest that remains and will remain unbroken through eternity, into which even now the trusting soul enters by faith.

In the third division, which is by far the longest, we have the very heart of this wonderful epistle. The heavenly sanctuary is here opened to the eye of faith, and there within the veil our Lord Jesus Christ is seen officiating as our Great High Priest, touched with the feeling of our infirmities, ministering to all the needs of His saints on earth, and yet ever giving them a perfect representation before the Throne of God. His priesthood is unchangeable because, properly speaking, it begins on the resurrection side of death. Having died for our sins upon the cross, He now lives to die no more, so He will never be superseded by another priest. Nor is His priesthood after the Aaronic or Levitical order. He is both King and Priest at one time after the order of Melchisedek; but be it carefully observed, after the *pattern* of Aaron. The instruction given in the Old Testament concerning the Aaronic priesthood was all designed to picture His glorious person and wondrous work.

Having settled the sin question on earth, He has passed through the created heavens into the Holiest, the immediate dwelling-place of God, and there has taken His seat as our Forerunner, our Intercessor, and as the Mediator of the New Covenant. The veil which of old separated the Holy Place from the Holiest of all, picturing the flesh of Christ, was rent in His death, and now the way is open for God to come out to man and for man to go in to God. In Christ, man has already entered in, for He is the archetypal Man, the firstborn among many brethren who shall all eventually be conformed to His blessed image, having the same title to enter in as He Himself has, namely, His personal perfection and His finished work.

Solemn are the warnings given in this great division, in chapters 6 and 10, against the terrible possibility of apostasy, to which many from among the Jews who professed faith in Jesus as their Messiah, but had never really trusted Him as their Savior, were especially liable. Any one who has had much experience in dealing with troubled souls knows that Satan has often used these passages to the sore distraction of uninstructed people of sensitive conscience, who have not learned to distinguish between apostasy and backsliding. And the attempted explanations that some, who should know better, have given of these warnings have only made confusion worse confounded. We shall examine them all in detail in their proper connection. But here it may be well to say that no born-again person will ever become an apostate, for the indwelling Holy Spirit will guard him from that dreadful state. Backsliding is another thing altogether, and probably few of us realize how often we are guilty of it. Any Christian who is not at the present time enjoying Christ as much as he did in a past day, or living for God as devotedly as he once did, is just to that extent a backslider. The word itself is, of course, not a New Testament term at all. We find it only once in the Bible, in Proverbs 14:14. There we read, "The backslider in heart shall be filled with his own ways." The word *backsliding* is found many times, though only in Jeremiah and Hosea. But while these terms are not found in the New Testament, we have many warnings against the state of soul to which they apply, and it is only too evident that the experience of backsliding is most common. How great the mercy of God that bears with our manners in the wilderness and restores our souls when we wander from Him!

When we come to the fourth division, what a delight it is to see how God discerns the least evidence of faith working in the souls of His people. In this wonderful honor roll of the eleventh chapter, what lessons are unfolded, designed by God to spur us on to tread the same path of faith in the power of the Holy Spirit, looking unto Jesus.

And this is what the fifth division really emphasizes, for it gives us the practical ways that should characterize those who have believed the truth set forth in this epistle. It makes it clear too, that the great object in writing it was to separate those who believed in the Lord Jesus from the temple and the synagogue, leading them outside the camp of a religious system that God had set to one side, to find in Christ alone the satisfying portion of their souls.

It will be observed that after each unfolding of truth, the Spirit of God gives a special warning lest having heard with the outward ear, the truth may not have entered the heart, and there may be a slipping away from it and a drifting back to a religious system that has nothing to offer a sinner seeking a purged conscience and desiring to enter into the presence of God in peace. These warnings had special application to the Hebrews of apostolic days who had heard the gospel and were intellectually convinced that Jesus was the promised Messiah, but who were ever in danger of mistaking outward adherence to His cause for heart-acceptance of Christ as their Savior, as, alas, many do today. It is quite possible to believe the Scripture records, accept their historicity and acknowledge the Messiahship of Jesus, with the conscience unexercised and no evidence of repentance unto life whatsoever; therefore the importance of giving heed to the warnings as well as to the truth unfolded here.

Professing Christians today are in no real sense in exactly the same position as those who in the first Christian centuries had turned away from Judaism and declared themselves followers of Jesus, the Messiah, and were sorely tempted, because of the severe persecutions to which they were exposed, to recant and go back to the ancient religious system. Yet how many there are in Christendom who take the place of being followers of our Lord and Savior, but who in the hour of testing are in grave peril lest through undervaluing the great truths of the gospel they never go further than a mere intellectual acquiescence in the ethical precepts of Christianity, knowing nothing of the new birth and the saving power of the blood of Christ. It is easy for such to profess to hold what they are pleased to denominate "The Religion of Jesus" while repudiating the atoning work of the cross and His High Priestly intercession, both of which are of no value whatever unless He be what the Scriptures declare Him to be, the Son of God in all reality, as well as Son of Man. "What think ye of Christ?" is still the great and abiding test.

As we study this epistle together, may we indeed see in Him the One who has fulfilled all the shadows of the legal dispensation and is the satisfying portion of all who turn to Him as repentant sinners, trusting Him alone for their eternal redemption.

CHAPTER 1

The Glories of the Son of God

Hebrews 1:1–2:4

God Speaking in the Son (Heb. 1:1–4)

God, who at sundry times and in divers manners spake in time past unto the fathers by the prophets, hath in these last days spoken unto us by his Son, whom he hath appointed heir of all things, by whom also he made the worlds; who being the brightness of his glory, and the express image of his person, and upholding all things by the word of his power, when he had by himself purged our sins, sat down on the right hand of the Majesty on high: being made so much

> better than the angels, as he hath by inheritance obtained a more excellent name than they.

As we begin our study of this sublime epistle, we are brought face to face with God Himself, ever yearning for the love and confidence of the race created in His own image and after His own likeness, but which in the person of its first head was scarcely placed in a position of authority before departing from the Creator, obedience to whom ever means blessing, and disobedience means misery and remorse. Sin had no sooner come into the world than God came in grace seeking the sinner, and so from the first question, "Adam, where art thou?" on to the incarnation, God has been speaking to man. In many places and in many ways in former times, He made known His mind through divinely inspired men, prophets who "spoke as they were moved by the Holy Spirit." But while in this way God was revealed in measure, that revelation could be, in the nature of things, only fragmentary. Now in the fullness of times, at the end of the probationary ages, in these days of blessing, He has spoken to us not through a mere human agency, but in the person of the Son. In other words, it is not now God sending a messenger to man to make known His will and to call him back to Himself, but it is God coming out to man in the Son. This is the same as that of which the apostle John speaks in the first chapter of his Gospel, verses 14 and 18: "And the Word was made flesh, and dwelt among us (and we beheld his glory, the glory as of the only begotten of the Father,) full of grace and truth. . . . No man hath seen God at any time; the only begotten Son, which is in the bosom of the Father, he hath declared him." God is no longer hidden nor at a distance. He has come down into His own world seeking those who have wandered from Him, manifesting Himself in all His infinite holiness and righteousness and yet with all His matchless love and compassion. In Christ, God is fully told out. None need say now, "Oh, that I knew where I might find Him!" or, "Show us the Father and it sufficeth us," for the Eternal Son who became flesh to make

God known has said, "He that hath seen Me hath seen the Father. I and My Father are one."

It is of all importance that we grasp this tremendous fact. The Son is one with the Father and with the Spirit. All are coequal and co-eternal. When the Son became incarnate, He was the same person that He had been from eternity, but by His incarnation He took humanity into union with Deity and so became Son in a new sense as Man born of a virgin. Having no human father, God alone was the Father of His humanity as truly as of His Deity. I admit the awkwardness of the last expression, but this is a mystery almost unlawful for man to utter, and of necessity our poor language is a most imperfect vehicle to convey to the mind such sublime truths. Yet there can be no question as to the truths themselves, for one who accepts the testimony of the Word of God.

It is the Son whom God has established Heir of all things. This, of course, refers to Him as having become Man, for it is as Man He will rule a redeemed universe in righteousness. But the apostle immediately adds, "By whom also He made the worlds," and this brings us face to face with God Himself, God the Creator of all things. It is the same person who made the universe who will reign over it. It is interesting to note that the original for "worlds" is here literally "ages" (*tous aionas*), an expression which actually means the "time worlds," but as is well known, was frequently used for the universe. Perhaps it might be correct to say, "By Him also the ages were fitted together"; that is, Christ the Son is the center of all God's thoughts, and it is He who planned the ages and who created the world upon, or in which, the dispensations would be manifested.

He is the forth-shining of the divine splendor, or the effulgence of His glory. J. N. Darby, in commenting on this word *effulgence*, speaks of it as that which "fully presents the glory which is in something else, [as] light makes us know what the sun is; the tabernacle, what the pattern in the mount was."[1] So as we become acquainted with the Lord Jesus as set before us in the Gospels, we learn what God is in all His fullness. For Christ is the exact expression of His character, or as we have it in our version, "the express image of His person." It is the divine character perfectly manifested in the Man Christ Jesus. This is the very opposite to the modern thought of an apotheosis. Jesus was not a Godlike Man, striving after holiness and piety. He was God Himself come down to earth in flesh, reconciling the world unto Himself. Nothing like this is known in any human religious system. It is unique because it is divine, and divine because it is unique. Man could easily think of becoming God. This was the Devil's lie at the beginning, "Ye shall be as Elohim," and is the foundation principle of all false religious systems. In Christianity alone do we learn that God became Man, and this for our redemption.

He who was crucified through weakness was the One who, at that very moment, was "upholding all things by the word of His power." Never for one instant did He take His hand off the control bar of the universe. What a marvelous suggestion of power there is in these words, and how our thoughts of Him are magnified as we realize who it was who stooped in grace to make purification of sins!

It is evident that the ordinary version does not quite give the thought here. We read, "Having by Himself purged our sins"; but there are many whose sins are not purged, and this the epistle to the Hebrews clearly takes into account. The words "by Himself" are not found in the original at all, but they are implied because the verb is in the middle voice, which reflects the action back upon the subject. On the other hand, the word "our" must be omitted altogether. It is the act of making an available means for purgation that is here stressed, "Having accomplished the purification of sins (by Himself)." That is, upon the cross He finished the work whereby the sin question is settled to the divine satisfaction, so that that question, as such, no longer comes up between God and men, but all who trust in Him are, upon the basis of that work, actually purified or purged from all their sins before God.

This work having been completed, He took His seat as Man on the right hand of the eternal Majesty on high. None but a divine person could sit down there upon the throne of the universe. But there He sits as entitled to share that throne with His Father. And He is there, be it observed, as Man in a glorified body, but a real body nevertheless, the same body that was nailed to the cross and that lay in Joseph's tomb, but now transfigured as when His disciples beheld Him upon the Holy Mount.

> Now seated on Jehovah's throne,
> The Lamb once slain, in glory bright,
> 'Tis thence Thou watchest o'er Thine own,
> Guarding them through the deadly fight.
> —Fanny Theodora Wigram

So by taking this place, He has made it manifest that His is a name far more excellent than that of any created angel. They are but ministers and servants. He is Son. Here for the first time we get the word *better*, a term that occurs frequently in this epistle as already indicated. The Son is so much better than the angels because by inheritance He has a name superior to their names. It is not what He wins by His devotedness, it is that which is His by right because of His relationship to the Father from eternity.

The Son Greater than the Angels (Heb. 1:5–14)

> For unto which of the angels said he at any time, Thou art my Son, this day have I begotten thee? And again, I will be to him a Father, and he shall be to me a Son? And again, when he bringeth in the firstbegotten into the world, he saith, And let all the angels of God worship him. And of the angels he saith, Who maketh his angels spirits, and his ministers a flame of fire. But unto the Son he saith, Thy throne, O God, is for ever and ever: a sceptre of righteousness is the sceptre of thy kingdom. Thou hast loved righteousness, and hated iniquity; therefore God, even thy God, hath anointed thee with the oil of gladness above thy fellows. And, Thou, Lord,

> in the beginning hast laid the foundation of the earth; and the heavens are the works of thine hands: they shall perish; but thou remainest; and they all shall wax old as doth a garment; and as a vesture shalt thou fold them up, and they shall be changed: but thou art the same, and thy years shall not fail. But to which of the angels said he at any time, Sit on my right hand, until I make thine enemies thy footstool? Are they not all ministering spirits, sent forth to minister for them who shall be heirs of salvation?

The apostle here proceeds to marshal an array of Old Testament Scripture passages to show the superiority of the Son to the angels, and to prove particularly to those who, like his Jewish readers, reverence the Old Testament, that He is not teaching anything contrary to what was therein revealed.

Let us look at these Scripture passages in order. The first one gives us His incarnation. The quotation is from Psalm 2:7: "Thou art my Son; this day have I begotten thee." The expression "this day" forbids the thought that it is eternal generation that is here referred to, true as that is. It is as begotten of the virgin that the Father addresses Him as Son. I know it is sometimes said that the reference is to His resurrection, based upon the authorized reading of Acts 13:33, where we read, "He hath raised up Jesus again; as it is also written in the second psalm," etc. But the word "again" is an interpolation as any carefully edited text would show. It is simply: He has raised up Jesus, in accordance with the words, "Thou art my Son, this day have I begotten thee," thus agreeing perfectly with the angel's message to the blessed virgin Mary: "That holy thing which shall be born of thee shall be called the Son of God."

In the second quotation we have His walk of faith here upon the earth: "I will be to him a Father, and he shall be to me a Son." This is evidently the promise made to David as recorded in 2 Samuel 7:14 and celebrated in Psalm 89. At first sight, it might seem to have reference to Solomon, but it is evident that a greater than Solomon was in view, He who even from His childhood could say, "Wist ye not that I must be about my Father's business?"

The third quotation is taken from Psalm 97:7, where it is rendered, "Worship him, all ye gods." This psalm celebrates Messiah's triumph over all the enemies of Jehovah and His appearing in glory to reign over all the nations. The reference is clearly, I take it, to His second coming. It is not exactly, "When he brought his first begotten into the world," but "when He brings" Him again into the inhabited earth. In that day all will recognize Him as the supreme object of worship. In contrast to this, it is said of the angels in Psalm 104:4, "Who maketh his angels spirits; his ministers a flaming fire." They are created beings, and never occupy any other place than that of servants.

The next two verses are taken from Psalm 45, where in verse 6 we have before us the Eternal Son, and in verse 7 the Son become Man. In the first instance He is directly addressed by the Father as God from eternity: "Unto the Son he saith, thy throne, O God, is forever and ever; a sceptre of righteousness is the sceptre of thy kingdom." He is called directly "The God" (*Ho Theos*). It would be impossible to indicate His full deity in any more conclusive way than this. But the next verse shows that He has walked through this world as Man, displaying the divine character, loving righteousness and hating iniquity. And as Man, God is His God and has now anointed Him with the oil of gladness above His companions.

The next quotation requires most careful attention in order not to miss the force of it. It is taken from Psalm 102:25–27. In verses 23 and 24 of that psalm, the Son is heard addressing the Father in view of the cross. He cries, "He weakened my strength in the way; he shortened my days. I said, O my God, take me not away in the midst of my days: thy years are throughout all generations." The verses that follow might seem at first glance to be a continuation of His plea, but with the light that this divinely inspired commentary throws upon them, we see that they are the answer of the Father to the Son. God replies to the Sufferer of Calvary: "Of old hast thou laid the foundation of the earth: and the heavens are the work of thy hands. They shall perish, but thou shalt endure: yea, all of them shall wax old like a garment; as a vesture shalt thou change them, and they shall be changed: but thou art the same, and thy years shall have no end."

Thus the apostle has established the full deity of our Blessed Lord in contrast with whom angels, however glorious, are but creatures, ministering spirits sent forth to minister for them who shall be heirs of salvation, and who themselves worship the Son of God.

The Importance of Receiving and Holding Fast the Truth as to the Person of the Son (Heb. 2:1–4)

> Therefore we ought to give the more earnest heed to the things which we have heard, lest at any time we should let them slip. For if the word spoken by angels was steadfast, and every transgression and disobedience received a just recompense of reward; how shall we escape, if we neglect so great salvation; which at the first began to be spoken by the Lord, and was confirmed unto us by them that heard him; God also bearing them witness, both with signs and wonders, and with divers miracles, and gifts of the Holy Ghost, according to his own will?

We have here a solemn warning addressed to all to whom the truth of Christ's superiority to angels has come, impressing upon them the importance of giving earnest attention to these things lest at any time they should drift past them, or lest they should seem to run out as from leaking vessels. It is one thing to accept the truth intellectually and profess adherence to certain doctrines. It is another thing to receive the truth in the heart and thus to be born of God. The danger for these Hebrews was that they might have allied themselves with the Christian company outwardly while never having actually received the truth in their hearts, by which means alone they could be regenerated. There was always the danger that under the stress of persecution such professors might give up or drift away from what was of prime importance—a true confession of Christ. And so they were warned that, as of old when God gave the law (for that is the word spoken by angels referred to in v. 2), "every transgression and disobedience received a just recompense of reward," even though the people had declared their adherence to all that God had spoken; so now, how shall we escape if we are careless regarding so great salvation? Great, because of the dignity of the person who accomplished it, proclaimed first by the Lord Himself when here in the world, and later confirmed by His apostles! God had set His seal to their testimony by giving them the power to work mighty signs and wonders, as promised in Mark 16 and elsewhere. These signs followed them as they went everywhere preaching the Word, the Holy Spirit working miraculously through them to accredit the gospel message. To turn away from Christianity would mean to blaspheme against the Holy Spirit, for they could not reject the testimony thus accredited without denying the work of the Holy Spirit. If the mighty signs were not wrought by Him, who then was their author? They must acknowledge that the Holy Spirit was bearing witness to the truth of the gospel, or, as their fathers had done, impute these wonders to the power of Satan.

Notice that the gifts of the Spirit were according to His own will. This is important, and it is in accord with what is written in 1 Corinthians 12, concerning spiritual gifts, where we are told, "But all these worketh that one and the selfsame Spirit, dividing to every man severally as he will" (v. 11). If this were better understood, there would be less insistence upon certain gifts as evidences of the Spirit's indwelling.

CHAPTER 2

The Glories and Humiliation of the Son of Man

Hebrews 2:5–4:13

Having considered our Blessed Lord from the standpoint of His deity, both as the Eternal Son and as the Son of God in manhood, we are now called upon to think of Him in His humiliation as He entered into the experiences of humanity in order that He might become the Captain of our salvation. We should never forget that His humanity is as real as His deity. He was born of a virgin; a babe, to all outward appearances like any other, and a perfectly normal child, growing up from infancy to manhood, increasing in wisdom as He increased in stature, and a sharer in all that pertained to human nature as originally created by God. And He has gone up to heaven as Man, so that we may properly sing: "He wears our nature on the throne."

But let us never forget His human nature was sinless throughout as was that of Adam before the fall. He did not come under Adam's federal headship and so did not inherit his fallen estate. God alone was His Father, as we have already seen, and as Scripture abundantly bears witness.

But inasmuch as He was both God and Man in one person, His humanity was not only innocent as was that of the first man, which was therefore subject to failure, but it was holy, repelling evil, for He was the second Man, the Lord from heaven. This precludes all possibility of sin or failure on His part.

Nevertheless, He entered into our human condition and circumstances, not when the race was unfallen but after the fall, when it had become bruised and battered by sin. So He passed, Himself sinless, through this life exposed to pain and sorrow, to hunger and weariness, to trial and temptation, and entered fully into all human experiences which did not involve personal demerit, dying at last upon a felon's cross where Jehovah laid upon Him the iniquity of us all. While there was no sin in Him, our sins were made to meet upon Him, and He made full expiation for all our iniquities that we might be reconciled to God and justified from all things.

The Glory of the Son of Man and His Authority (Heb. 2:5–9)

> For unto the angels hath he not put in subjection the world to come, whereof we speak. But one in a certain place testified, saying, What is man, that thou art mindful of him? or the son of man, that thou visitest him? Thou madest him a little lower than the angels; thou crownedst him with glory and honour, and didst set him over the works of thy hands: thou

> hast put all things in subjection under his feet. For in that he put all in subjection under him, he left nothing that is not put under him. But now we see not yet all things put under him. But we see Jesus, who was made a little lower than the angels for the suffering of death, crowned with glory and honour; that he by the grace of God should taste death for every man.

While angels are greater in power and might than man in his present circumstances, they remain but servants. It was never God's purpose that the angels should be rulers over humanity. During the present age and throughout past dispensations, it has pleased God to use angels as His messengers in conveying His will to man. These glorious beings appeared to the patriarchs either to announce blessing or to warn of judgment. The law was given by the disposition of angels. By angelic guidance, the people of Israel were led through the wilderness, and during all the years of the theocracy angels appeared from time to time as representatives of the throne of God. When our blessed Lord Himself was here on earth angels came to minister unto Him, and when He comes into the world again, as we have seen in chapter 1, they will all worship Him. But it is not in the plan of God that they should administer the affairs of the divine government when the kingdom is actually established. "Unto the angels hath He not put in subjection the age to come." Notice it is "age," not "world"; that is, it is not the cosmos as such that is in view, but the coming age of righteousness when the kingdoms of this world will become the kingdoms of our Lord and of His Christ.

No angel will rule in that day. But He whose glory was foretold in the eighth Psalm will take the kingdom and rule in righteousness, for the certain place referred to in verse 6 is, as we know, Psalm 8:4–6, which is quoted here: "What is man, that thou art mindful of him? and the son of man, that thou visitest him? For thou hast made him a little lower than the angels, and hast crowned him with glory and honour. Thou madest him to have dominion over the works of thy hands; thou hast put all things under his feet." If we turn back to the psalm we might not realize that it is Christ who is in view, particularly as we notice verses 7–8 where all cattle and wild beasts, as well as fowls of the air and the fish of the sea, are said to be subjected to man. It might look as though it is but a confirmation of the Lord's word to Adam the first, to whom He said, "Be fruitful, and multiply, and replenish the earth, and subdue it: and have dominion over the fish of the sea, and over the fowl of the air, and over every living thing that moveth upon the earth" (Gen. 1:28). But we know well that Adam forfeited his headship through sin, and now in the eighth psalm that headship is confirmed to One who is called the Son of Man, which Adam, of course, never was. The apostle's use of the passage here in Hebrews makes it plain that it is the Last Adam to whom the psalm refers.

And so, as we read these words, we think of Him who delighted in the title "Son of Man" because it speaks of Him as the appointed ruler over the whole earth, who is to deliver it from the bondage of corruption. He was made a little lower than the angels, that is, He became Man, and men in their present condition are inferior to angels, though when redemption is completed, we shall have a place higher than angels can ever aspire to. And already He who took that place of humility has been received up into heaven as Man and crowned with glory and honor, and by divine fiat set over all creation. For God has appointed Him Heir of all things and decreed that all shall be in subjection under His feet. He leaves nothing unsubjected to Him. His place is that of supreme authority.

But as we look around the world today, can we think for a moment that His authority is being exercised? "We see not yet all things put under Him," and though many centuries have passed since this epistle to the Hebrews was written, rebellion against God still characterizes this lower universe. The divine law is flouted. The grace of God is despised. His Word is refused. His Holy Spirit is ignored. His people are still called upon to suffer for righteousness' sake. Surely all things are not yet put under Him! Such might well be the natural conclusion to which we would come if we looked only upon the things that are seen.

But when by the eye of faith, through the telescope of the Word, we pierce the heavens, we see Jesus, who once became a little lower than the angels with the view to the suffering of death, even now crowned with glory and honor. He sits exalted on the throne of the Eternal as a glorified Man at the right hand of the Majesty on high. God has set Him above all things, which is conclusive proof to us that all things shall yet be subjected to Him.

Notice the special reason given for His humiliation. He became a little lower than the angels for the suffering of death: that is, with this very object in view. It was impossible that Deity as such should die. If He would taste death for every man, He must become Man, for only as Man could He die. This is the mystery set forth in that ancient type in Leviticus 14:5 where, in connection with the cleansing of the leper, the priest was instructed to take two birds alive and clean. One of the birds was to be killed in an earthen vessel over running water. The other was to be dipped in the blood of the dead bird and let loose in the open field. The two birds typified one Christ. The first speaks of Him as the Heavenly One who entered into the earthen vessel of humanity in order that He might die. The second speaks of Him as the Risen One who has returned to the heavens in all the value of His own most precious blood.

Then it is well to notice that after all it is not merely for every *man* that He tasted death. The context makes it plain that the "all" for which He died is in the neuter in the original. It might rightly be rendered, "that He by the grace of God should taste death for everything." For through His death not only will sinners be saved and the world of redeemed men brought into eternal blessing, but the creation itself shall be delivered from the bondage of corruption and everything in heaven and earth at last brought into harmony with God. None shall fail of this reconciliation excepting those who deliberately prefer their sins to the salvation so freely offered.

The Perfecting of the Captain of Our Salvation Through Suffering (Heb. 2:10–18)

This section is one of the most precious in all the epistle and requires careful consideration, for there is grave danger of misunderstanding some of its great declarations unless we are familiar with what the Word of God elsewhere reveals concerning the person and work of the Lord Jesus.

If He would become Captain of our salvation—or, literally, File-leader of our salvation, the One who is Himself the Way of Life and leads us in that Way—He must be perfected through sufferings. But notice how His glory as Creator is insisted on when His sufferings are in view. "It became Him," that is, it was consistent under the circumstances for Him, "for whom are all things and by whom are all things"—the same as in Colossians, "All things were created by Him and for Him"—if He would bring many sons into glory (and this we know is the very reason for which He came into the world), to be made perfect, not as to His character, but as to His Saviorhood, by sufferings. There was never any imperfection in Him as Man. He was always the Perfect One, but let it never be forgotten that the perfect life of Jesus would never have saved one poor sinner. In order to become Captain of salvation, that He might lead many sons to glory, He must go by way of Gethsemane and Golgotha, where He was perfected by sufferings. Apart from His bitter passion, there could be no redemption for lost men and women.

And in verse 11 we have the glorious result of His sufferings. "Both he that sanctifieth and they who are sanctified are all of one." To sanctify is to separate, to set apart. He set Himself apart in order that He might become our Savior. "For their sakes I sanctify myself, that they also might be sanctified through the truth" (John 17:19). And now, having gone back to the glory from whence He came, He is Himself the Sanctifier of all His own. He has been made unto us wisdom, even righteousness, sanctification, and redemption. Every believer has been set apart by Him and in Him to God the Father, and so it can be said of Him and of us, "We are all of one." That is, I take it, all of one Father or of one family. And therefore He is not ashamed to call us brethren. Our poor hearts cannot but realize how worthless we have been and are, and how, if He were any other than He is, He might well be ashamed to own such as we as His brethren. But we have become partakers of His divine life, a life that is eternal and to which sin can never attach. And so He owns us gladly as His brethren, though, may I add, nowhere in Scripture is He spoken of as our brother. He says, "Ye call me Master and Lord, and ye say well, for so I am" (John 13:13). But He whom we gladly own as Lord, in wondrous grace calls us His brothers.

In Psalm 22 we see Him hanging on the cross, the Forsaken One, drinking the wormwood and the gall, bearing the judgment due to our sins. In verses 1–21 of that psalm He is seen alone, suffering at the hands of God what our guilt deserved. Then from verse 22 on He is no longer alone, but as the Risen One is surrounded by multitudes who owe their salvation to His sufferings on the tree, and it is in resurrection He exclaims: "I will declare thy name unto my brethren: in the midst of the congregation will I praise thee." This is the passage that is quoted in verse 12 of our chapter; but for "congregation" we have the word "church," a translation, as we know, of the Greek *ekklesia*, which was the Septuagint rendering for the Hebrew term translated "congregation." It is the assembly of the redeemed, and in the midst of that assembly the Risen Christ takes His place as the Chief Chorister leading the praises of His people's hearts.

He once trod the path of faith Himself, as implied in the quotation, in verse 13, from Isaiah 8:17, "I will put my trust in him." As Man here on earth, He walked through the wilderness of this world with perfect confidence in the Father, looking on to the time when, surrounded by all His own, He could say, as quoted from the eighteenth verse of the same chapter, "Behold, I and the children whom the Lord hath given me." But it is not to Isaiah and his children that these words primarily apply. The prophet of old was but the type of the Lord Himself who spoke by the Spirit through Isaiah.

In Hebrews 2:14–15 we read: "Forasmuch then as the children are partakers of flesh and blood, he also himself likewise took part of the same; that through death he might destroy him that had the power of death, that is, the devil; and deliver them who through fear of death were all their lifetime subject to bondage." It is necessary to give the most careful consideration to what is really stated here lest we, even though unintentionally, detract from the glory of the humanity of our blessed Lord. A casual reading of the first part of verse 14 might suggest that our Savior participated in everything that is connected with flesh and blood. Indeed, this has been the teaching of many. According to them, the Son of God assumed humanity with all its sinfulness and all its limitations of ignorance, so that even though they acknowledge that in some sense He was truly God manifest in flesh, yet with them it is Deity enshrouded in poor, degraded, sinful, human nature; unable, therefore, to make Himself known in His fullness. But what we are really told here is that inasmuch as the children of faith are human beings, not angels, as the writer points out in verse 16, so in order that He might be the true *Goel* or Kinsman-Redeemer, He in infinite grace became Man and thus took part of the same human nature. This does not in any sense imply that He took defiled human nature. This the Holy Spirit guarded against in the fullest possible way, so that the angel could say to Mary, "That holy thing which shall be born of thee shall be called the Son of God." While in our English version the words "partakers of" and "took part of" might seem to imply in each instance fullest participation, the original does not necessarily imply this. The following note from the pen of F. W. Grant, the most spiritual expositor I know, is very helpful.

> It must be noted here, as it often has been, that while the children are said to be partakers of flesh and blood—this "partaking" being a real having in common, a participation of the most thorough kind—in His own "taking part" another word is used which implies limitation. It does not indeed show the character of the limitation; but the difference between the words makes us necessarily ask what, in fact, that limitation was; and the answer comes to us immediately, that while His was true humanity in every particular necessary to constitute it that, yet humanity as men have it, the humanity of *fallen* men, was *not* His. Here there must be strict limitation. We must add, as the apostle does afterward with regard to His temptation, "sin apart." Sin, with the consequences of sin, He could not take. Death could have no power over Him, except as He might submit Himself voluntarily to it, and this He did; but it was obedience to His Father's will, and no necessity of His condition, as it is of ours.[1]

And if it be remembered that sin is not inherent in human nature as such, but that it is a foreign thing brought in through the fall, it can be readily understood how it could be said that our blessed Lord "took part of the same" without involving full participation in all that had come in through man's failure. He must be the Unblemished One if He would make satisfaction for sins. It is through failure to realize this that many very wrong systems have been built up teaching the sinfulness of Christ's humanity, something which one would expect would be repugnant to every truly converted person.

Having thus become Man, though sinless, our Lord became man's Champion and went forth as our David to destroy or annul the great Goliath who had terrorized the world ever since the fall, "him that had the power of death, that is, the Devil." The cross was for Christ a Valley of Elah where He met our cruel foe and put an end to his authority over the souls of all who believe the gospel, thus delivering us even now, who in times past through fear of death were held in bitter bondage all our lives. Satan is a conquered foe and no believer need now fear him, but it is incumbent on us to watch and pray lest he mislead us and hinder our communion with God, though he well knows he can never destroy our life.

The sixteenth verse seems to be unfortunately rendered in our King James Version, through a translation that implies that it is a question of nature that is under consideration. A better translation reads as follows: "For truly he taketh not hold of angels, but of the seed of Abraham he took hold" (author's translation). That is, Christ did not come to be the Savior of fallen angels. They are shut up unto eternal darkness, but in infinite grace He passed angels by and laid hold on the seed of Abraham, that is, on all who believe in Him. In order to do this, it was necessary that He should be made like unto His brethren, as we have already seen, that thus having passed sinlessly through all human experiences, He might be a merciful and faithful High Priest in things pertaining to God, to make—not "reconciliation," as in the King James Version text, but—expiation or atonement for the sins of the people. In this we see the fulfillment of the type of the great Day of Atonement when the high priest first offered the sacrifice at the altar and then presented the blood in the Holiest. So our Lord, at the close of His pilgrim path, on our behalf offered up Himself upon the cross to make expiation, atonement, or propitiation, for our sins. The original word is that used in the Septuagint Version of the Old Testament to translate the Hebrew word for atonement. Reconciliation is the result of this, but it is we who are reconciled to God, not He who has to be reconciled to us.

And now our Great High Priest lives on high ever ready to succor them that are tempted. Having Himself suffered being tempted, His heart goes out in compassion to us in our great need. Note the contrast between this passage and 1 Peter 4:1. Here in Hebrews we read that Christ "suffered being tempted." In 1 Peter we are told that "He that hath suffered in the flesh hath ceased from sin." This brings out most vividly the difference between Christ's perfect humanity and our sinful natures. To us, sin is attractive and alluring. We suffer in the flesh when we resist it. With Him it was the very opposite. Temptation caused Him the keenest suffering. It was the presentation of that to His holy soul which He abhorred, and even to have to do with it, in the sense of temptation, caused Him pain and anguish.

The Glory of the Son over the House of God (Heb. 3:1–6)

Having thus introduced Christ Jesus as High Priest of our confession, we are now bidden to consider Him in that character as the Apostle of the new dispensation. It is Christ who has superseded both Moses and Aaron. Moses was the apostle of the separated people who were partakers of an earthly calling, and Aaron was their high priest. But Jesus is both the Apostle and High Priest of the holy brethren; holy, as we have already seen, because set apart to God in Him, and thus partakers of the heavenly calling.

He is infinitely superior to Moses because Moses, though faithful in his day, was simply a servant in the house of God, but Christ Jesus is the Builder of the house and is Son over His own house, whose house are we, if we hold fast the confidence and the rejoicing of the hope firm unto the end. Observe that the term "house" is used here in three senses. The house in which Moses was faithful was the tabernacle. But the tabernacle was the pattern of things in the heavens, so the house that God built is the universe. But the house over which Christ is set and to which we belong is that building composed of living stones in which every believer has a place.

And now we have the first word of warning, lest in cherishing a temporary confidence we seem to be animated by the joy that hope in Christ gives, and yet, after all, are lacking in a faith that is genuine. The *if* in verse 6 is a test of profession. It was very possible then, and it is still, that men might mingle with a Christian company and find a certain amount of gladness and joy springing from an intellectual acquaintance with Christianity, who after all were not truly born of

God. Continuance proves the reality of our confession. This is further stressed in the portion that follows.

The Perfected Savior Leading His People Through the Wilderness to the Eternal Sabbath of God: Warning as to Coming Short (Heb. 3:7–4:13)

In this lengthy section the warning is continued and is based upon Israel's experiences of old. Just as their fathers had left Egypt a great multitude, yet many (in fact, the majority) failed to enter the land of Canaan because of unbelief; so a vast throng of Jews had become outwardly obedient to the faith, but there was ever the danger that their conversion to Christianity might be merely intellectual and their forsaking of Judaism simply what people sometimes call today "a change of religion." Therefore the importance of examining themselves in the light of the Word of God and pressing on to "make their calling and election sure," as the apostle Peter elsewhere puts it. We are saved entirely by grace, but we are created in Christ Jesus unto good works, as we read in Ephesians, and no one has a right to confess himself a Christian who is not seeking to live for the glory of God. If there be not a nature that delights in the will of God, there is every reason to doubt whether one has ever been truly saved.

And so we have here a warning word taken from Psalm 95:7–11: "For he is our God; and we are the people of his pasture, and the sheep of his hand. Today if ye will hear his voice, harden not your heart, as in the provocation, and as in the day of temptation in the wilderness: when your fathers tempted me, proved me, and saw my work. Forty years long was I grieved with this generation, and said, It is a people that do err in their heart, and they have not known my ways: unto whom I sware in my wrath that they should not enter into my rest." Notice how this quotation from the psalm is introduced, "As the Holy Ghost saith." It is not merely the word of David or some other unknown author, but it is the word of the Holy Spirit Himself warning those who profess the name of the Lord against hardening their hearts and walking in disobedience.

To these Hebrews the exhortation is given: "Take heed, brethren, lest there be in any of you an evil heart of unbelief, in departing from the living God. But exhort one another daily, while it is called today; lest any of you be hardened through the deceitfulness of sin. For we are made partakers [companions] of Christ, if we hold the beginning of our confidence steadfast unto the end" (vv. 12–14). Faith is manifested by a godly walk. Where there is lack of faith, the outward life may for a time seem to be consistent with the Christian profession, but eventually the old carnal nature will assert itself and there will be a turning back to the world; or, as in this case, to that mere carnal religion from which Christ would deliver. This second *if* is linked with verse 6, and again we are reminded that continuance in the walk of faith is the proof of a genuine Christian confession. In the last five verses of this third chapter, the Spirit of God uses the case of Israel in the wilderness as a solemn warning to all who now have professedly gone on a pilgrimage. The people who fell in the desert of old were those who believed not. They never entered into God's rest. Indeed, they could not do so because of their unbelief. That rest of course was Canaan, a type of the rest that remains for the people of God now.

The subject is continued in the first thirteen verses of chapter 4. "Let us therefore fear, lest, a promise being left us of entering into his rest, any of you should seem to come short of it" (v. 1). The rest here spoken of is not our present enjoyment of Christ, as many have imagined, but clearly refers to that rest which, as in Israel's case, is at the end of the way. What a solemn thing for any who eventually come short of that! The glad tidings of a rest to come, we have heard as did they. Let us then see that we profit thereby in a way which they did not, proving the reality of our faith by our behavior.

Then in verse 3 we have present rest as we truly believe God, and thus enjoy the rest of faith. The quotation from Psalm 95 is again referred to in order to show that the rest there spoken of could not refer merely to creation rest, for God entered into that centuries and millenniums before the psalm was written, as we read in Genesis 2:2: "He rested on the seventh day from all his work," but the psalm says, "If they shall enter into my rest," showing that the rest was still future. Nor was it merely Canaan rest, for they had long since reached Canaan, though those who did not believe failed of this. But another and a better rest is before the mind of the Spirit, for if Joshua had given them rest, God would not have spoken as though their rest was still in the future. It is well known that the name of our blessed Lord which we read as Jesus, is the Greek form of the Hebrew *Joshua*, so that Israel's great leader and our Great Savior both bore the same name. Joshua led those who believed into Canaan rest. Jesus leads those who believe into the present rest of faith and later into eternal rest. Both are brought before us in verses 9–11: "There remaineth therefore a rest to the people of God. For he that is entered into his rest, he also hath ceased from his own works, as God did from his. Let us labour therefore to enter into that rest, lest any man fall after the same example of unbelief." In verse 9 it is eternal rest, a Sabbath keeping that shall have no end, whereas verse 10 speaks of that rest which we now enter into and enjoy as "we walk by faith and not by sight." We are exhorted to be in earnest lest we even so much as seem to fall short of what is our proper portion in Christ.

And we need to remember that God's Word is ever the standard of judgment, and not our knowledge of it. Therefore the importance of becoming thoroughly conversant with the truth revealed in the Holy Scriptures. "For the word of God is quick, and powerful, and sharper than any twoedged sword, piercing even to the dividing asunder of soul and spirit, and of the joints and marrow, and is a discerner of the thoughts and intents of the heart. Neither is there any creature that is not manifest in his sight: but all things are naked and opened unto the eyes of him with whom we have to do" (vv. 12–13). We cannot but notice how intimately the written Word and the Eternal Word are linked together. It is clear that verse

12 is referring to revealed truth. This is the Word of God which is described as living and energetic, "sharper than any twoedged sword, piercing even to the dividing asunder of soul and spirit," that is, distinguishing between these two parts of the inward man; separating between "the joints and marrow," making a difference between what is outward and that which is hidden; and "is a discerner [*kritikos*] of the thoughts and intents of the heart." Men presume to criticize and to sit in judgment on the Word of God, but here we are told that the Word itself is the supreme critic of our inmost thoughts and inclinations. It is plain that throughout this twelfth verse it is the written Word that is in view, but in that which immediately follows we have the personal pronouns used, showing us that the Living Word is now before the soul, He from whom nothing is hidden but to whose all-seeing eyes everything is naked and open. How important that those who have to do with Him be real and true in all their ways!

CHAPTER 3

The Priesthood of the Heavenly Sanctuary Superior to That of Aaron

Hebrews 4:14–10:39

The Enthroned Priest After the Order of Melchisedek, Though of the Pattern of Aaron (Heb. 4:14–7:28)

We are now to consider the priesthood of Christ, a precious and wondrous theme meaning much for all believers during His present session at God's right hand in heaven, but something into which Jewish believers could enter with peculiar interest because of their former relationship to the earthly sanctuary and the high priesthood of Aaron and his sons.

There are those today who deny utterly Christ's priestly service on behalf of the church. They say (to use the exact language of one of the teachers of this school), "Christ is not my High Priest; He is a High Priest for Israel, not for the church which is His body. All believers now are part of the High Priest and it will be our place to intercede for Israel by and by." What an absurd obsession must he be laboring under who can use such language! Christ, the Head of the body, the church, is one aspect in which our blessed Lord is presented in the Word, but Christ as the High Priest is another aspect altogether. As members of the body we are seen in a peculiar relationship to Him which does not involve the thought of failure or infirmity. But as a pilgrim people passing through a sinful world, we have a Great High Priest ever representing us before God in heaven and ministering to our needs as they arise from moment to moment. To rob the Christian of this blessed truth is to leave him poor indeed. But that teaching is just part of an ultra-dispensational system which is soul-withering in the extreme, and occupies its votaries with fine distinctions that are often thoroughly unscriptural, instead of with Christ Himself and His work on our behalf.

The division upon which we now enter, extending from verse 14 of chapter 4 to verse 39 of chapter 10, is by far the largest part of the epistle. As already intimated, it opens up to us a vast system of precious truth, namely, the priesthood of the heavenly sanctuary, a priesthood far superior to the Aaronic system, not only because of the more excellent character of the Priest Himself, but because of the infinitely better sacrifice upon which it rests, the offering of the body of Jesus Christ once for all upon the cross for our sins.

Properly speaking, priesthood has to do with the heavens. Our blessed Lord was anointed to fulfill three offices—those of Prophet, Priest, and King. While to a certain extent these offices overlap, yet generally speaking we may say that He was Prophet on earth, He is Priest in heaven, and He will reign as King when He returns in glory. This, however, is not to deny that He was just as truly the King when He presented Himself to Israel in the days of His flesh. He was rejected in that special character when they exclaimed, "We have no king but Caesar," thus fulfilling the expression in the parable, "We will not have this man to reign over us." And so too it was as High Priest that He lifted up His eyes unto heaven and offered that wonderful intercessory prayer recorded in John 17. And as High Priest, fulfilling the type of the great day of atonement, He offered Himself to God as a sacrifice on our behalf. Then, too, we see Him in the role of Prophet when, on Patmos Isle, He appeared to the beloved apostle and gave him a marvelous revelation concerning things which must shortly come to pass.

The high priest of the Old Testament must of necessity be a man, one who could enter into the trials of his brethren, and so our Lord Jesus has already been demonstrated to be true Man as well as very God, that He might thus enter practically into all the sorrows and difficulties of His people. This is emphasized for us in the first section of the present division.

The Man in the Glory, Our Great High Priest (Heb. 4:14–5:10)

> Seeing then that we have a great high priest, that is passed into the heavens, Jesus the Son of God, let us hold fast our profession. For we have not an high priest which cannot be touched with the feeling of our infirmities; but was in all points tempted like as we are, yet without sin. Let us therefore come boldly unto the throne of grace, that we may obtain mercy, and find grace to help in time of need.
>
> For every high priest taken from among men is ordained for men in things pertaining to God, that he may offer both gifts and sacrifices for sins: who can have compassion on the ignorant, and on them that are out of the way; for that he himself also is compassed with infirmity. And by reason hereof he ought, as for the people, so also for himself, to

> offer for sins. And no man taketh this honour unto himself, but he that is called of God, as was Aaron. So also Christ glorified not himself to be made an high priest; but he that said unto him, Thou art my Son, today have I begotten thee. As he saith also in another place, Thou art a priest for ever after the order of Melchisedek. Who in the days of his flesh, when he had offered up prayers and supplications with strong crying and tears unto him that was able to save him from death, and was heard in that he feared; though he were a Son, yet learned he obedience by the things which he suffered; and being made perfect, he became the author of eternal salvation unto all them that obey him; called of God an high priest after the order of Melchisedek.

I have quoted the entire passage in order that we may not lose sight of the connection of its various parts. First observe that in verse 14 our Lord is spoken of as a Great High Priest, great in the dignity of His person and in the perfection of His character. He has passed into (or, literally, through) the heavens, as the high priest of old, having sacrificed at the altar, passed through the court and the Holy Place into the Holy of Holies. So our blessed Lord, having died upon the cross, has passed through the lower heavens surrounding this earth which we call the atmosphere, in which the birds fly, which are often spoken of as the birds of the heavens; on through the stellar heavens, the created universe stretching through apparently illimitable space; up and on into the heaven of heavens, the immediate dwelling place of God, where He has taken His seat as Man upon the eternal throne. There He sits exalted, Jesus the Son of God, the entire title speaking most blessedly of His humanity and divinity. In view of His session there at God's right hand, we are encouraged to hold fast our *confession*. It is generally recognized that this is a better translation than *profession*, as in the King James Version. We may *profess* what is not true. We *confess* what is real.

Our High Priest then is not One whose heart is indifferent to our circumstances; not One who cannot be touched with the feeling of our infirmities. He is as truly human as we, and in the days of His flesh He was tempted in all points like ourselves, though apart from sin. The expression, "yet without sin," has frequently been taken to mean, "yet without sinning," as though it simply implied that He did not fail when exposed to temptation, but the exact rendering would be "sin apart." That is, His temptations were entirely from without. He was never tempted by inbred sin as we are. He could say, "The prince of this world cometh and hath nothing in Me." When we are tempted from without, we have a traitor within who ever seeks to open the door of the citadel to the enemy. But it was otherwise with Him. If any ask, How then could His temptations be as real as ours? let us remember that when temptation was first presented to Adam and Eve, they were sinless beings, but being merely human, they yielded and plunged the race into ruin and disaster. Christ was not only innocent but holy, for He was God as well as Man.

"Tempted in all points" means of course that appeals were made to Him by Satan from the three standpoints whereby alone any of us can be tempted: "the lust of the flesh, the lust of the eyes, and the pride of life." Tempted on these three points, Eve capitulated completely. "She saw that the fruit of the tree was good for food"—the appeal to the lust of the flesh; "it was pleasant to the eye"—the appeal to the lust of the eye; "and a tree to be desired to make one wise"—the appeal to the pride of life. She failed on every point. To our Lord in the wilderness the same appeals were made. "Make these stones bread"—an appeal to fleshly desire; "he showed Him all the kingdoms of earth in a moment of time"—the lust of the eye; then in the suggestion that our Lord should cast Himself down from the pinnacle of the temple to be borne up by angels before the wondering eyes of the populace, we have the appeal to the pride of life. But He met every suggestion of evil by the Word of God. And now as the enthroned Conqueror, He sits exalted on the right hand of the Majesty on high, interceding for us, and we are bidden to come boldly unto the throne of grace there to obtain mercy because of failure, and find suited grace for seasonable help when exposed to temptation.

As we enter chapter 5 we are reminded that the high priest was taken from among men and set apart to minister on their behalf in things having to do with God. He was to present his brethren's gifts and sacrifices for sins. Note the distinction. On the cross our Lord presented the sacrifice for sins. In heaven now, He offers our gifts of worship and praise.

The earthly priest, because himself a man and as infirm as any of his brethren, could have compassion on the ignorant and on those who wandered from the path of rectitude. Conscious of his own failures, it was necessary that he should offer a propitiatory sacrifice for himself as well as for the people. In this we see the superiority of our Great High Priest, who needed no offering for Himself, but gave Himself in love for others.

In verse 4 we are reminded that no man was entitled to constitute himself a high priest. He became such by divine call, as in the case of Aaron who was chosen of God and set apart for this high office. Even so, Christ did not make Himself High Priest, but God the Father recognized Him as such when He declared in the words of Psalm 2:7, "Thou art my Son; this day have I begotten thee." His priesthood, however, was not of the Levitical order but of a different character altogether, even as it is written in Psalm 110:4, "Thou art a priest for ever after the order of Melchisedek." What is really involved in this we shall see when we come to consider chapter 7. It is enough to point out here that Melchisedek was recognized as priest of the most high God centuries before the Levitical priesthood came into existence. This latter, like the legal covenant with which it was connected, came in only "by the way," and had its place until the Son, who was to fulfill the Melchisedek type, should come.

In verses 7–10 the Spirit again emphasizes the reality of Christ's manhood and His participation in all the sinless experiences of His people. "In the days of his flesh," when He was here on earth in human condition, He trod the path of faith and took the place of dependence on the Father, "offered up prayers and supplications," accompanied by "strong crying and tears, unto him who was able to save him out of death." For, be it observed, He was not saved *from* dying nor did He ever pray to be saved from death, nor did He fear death. He came into the world to die, for that very purpose; but He was brought up from death, being raised by the power of God. What a testimony those tears were to the reality of His manhood! Three times we read of His weeping. He wept at the grave of Lazarus as He contemplated the awful ravages that death had made, tears of loving sympathy. He wept as He looked upon Jerusalem and His prophetic soul saw the tribulations through which the devoted city must pass. And He wept in Gethsemane's garden as His holy soul shrank from drinking the cup of divine indignation against sin, when He should hang upon the cross. While the cup could not be averted, nevertheless He was heard "for His piety," that is, not as some have said, in the removing of that which He feared, but rather because of His godly fear, His reverence for the Father's will. And thus He who is the Eternal Son who never knew what subjection meant, became Man, and as He trod the pilgrim path of suffering and rejection down here, He learned obedience by the things which He suffered. It is not that His will had to be subdued, but that from the moment when He assumed humanity He entered into new experiences, and He who had always commanded learned practically what obedience meant.

And thus being perfected as the Captain of Salvation, according to 2:10, which we have already considered, He has become the Author of eternal salvation unto all them who follow Him in the obedience of faith, having been saluted of God in resurrection as High Priest after the order of Melchisedek.

How carefully the Holy Spirit guards against the least suggestion of defilement in His nature while insisting upon the reality of His humanity. Great indeed is the mystery of godliness, for He, the Holy One, has been manifested in flesh. And now as the exalted Priest, He enters into all the sorrows of His people, sympathizing with them in all their infirmities. He does not sympathize with our sins, and indeed, we would not wish Him to, but He does feel for us in all our weakness and is waiting to supply needed strength for every trial.

Warning Against Apostasy: Safety Only in Resting upon the Word of God (Heb. 5:11–6:20)

We are now to consider one of those portions of the writings of "our beloved brother Paul," as Peter calls him, "wherein are some things hard to be understood, which those that are ignorant and unstable wrest to their own destruction." Probably there is no part of the Word of God that has stumbled immature and uninstructed Christians like that which is before us. Therefore the need of examining it with the utmost care.

The closing part of chapter 5, verses 11–14, is plain enough. Immediately upon bringing in the name of Melchisedek the apostle declares: "Of whom we have many things to say, and hard to be uttered, seeing ye are dull of hearing" (v. 11). The truth of the Melchisedek priesthood of our Lord Jesus would be most unpalatable to Jewish tastes, and difficult of apprehension where one was under legalistic bondage. We have only to consult the book of Acts, particularly in connection with Paul's last visit to Jerusalem, to realize how backward thousands of Hebrew believers were in the years immediately preceding the destruction of the Holy City and the manifest setting aside of the temple ritual. Those who, for the time that had elapsed since their conversion, ought to have been well able to teach others, were themselves needing instruction in the most elementary truths of the Word of God. They had not even grasped the distinction between Israel's hopes which are earthly, and those of the church which are heavenly. Neither had they realized the transitory and shadowy character of the Levitical economy in contrast with the permanency of the Christian revelation. They were ignorant of the first principles of the oracles of God, still requiring milk and unable to digest strong meat. They were babes in the truth when they should have been mature believers. The time had come to insist upon the setting aside of Judaism and going on to the full truth of Christianity. And so it is to this great step they are called as the sixth chapter opens.

Let us be very clear as to this. The urge of the Spirit here is not to leave earlier Christian experiences and go on to a deeper work of grace, as some put it. Neither is it to cease from being occupied with the elementary truths of Christianity and go on to deeper things. It is a call to leave the typical for the actual; the shadow for the substance; the partial revelation of Judaism (using this word in its very best sense) for the full unfolding of the truth of the new dispensation. Judaism is called "the word of the beginning of Christ," as in the marginal reading of the first part of verse 1. This of course includes the entire Mosaic revelation, the teaching of the prophets, and the ministry of John the Baptist. "The law and the prophets were until John, but now the kingdom of God is come and every man presseth into it." In six items the Spirit of God epitomizes these preliminary principles whereby the godly in Israel were prepared for the coming of the Christ. These are:

1. Repentance from dead works.

2. Faith toward God.

3. The doctrine of baptisms; or, literally, a teaching concerning ceremonial washings.

4. The laying on of hands (in connection with the sacrificial offerings).

5. Resurrection of the dead.

6. Eternal judgment.

Here then we have all that was basic in the former dispensation.

Throughout the Old Testament and in the ministry of John the Baptist, the people were called to repentance from dead works and urged to put their faith in God, the God of Israel. Through the ceremonial baptisms or washings of the law (as in 9:10, 13) the people were taught the need of cleansing, in order that they might have fellowship with God, a cleansing which was from physical defilement alone, "the putting away of the filth of the flesh," as Peter puts it. The laying on of hands has no reference whatever either to the laying on of the apostles' hands for the reception of the Holy Spirit as in Acts, or to ordination to the Christian ministry, as many have supposed. There is no *doctrine* of the laying on of hands to be found anywhere in the New Testament. Practice and doctrine are not the same thing. But under the Levitical economy when the offerer laid his hands upon the head of the sacrifice which was presented to God on his behalf, he was picturing a tremendous truth upon which this Epistle strongly insists. It was the identification of the offerer with the victim, and practically involved the transference of the offerer's sins to the offering which was put to death in the stead of the sinner. Resurrection of the dead is a cardinal Old Testament doctrine, denied indeed by worldly-minded Sadducees, but insisted upon by the Pharisees, and recognized by the apostle Paul as eminently scriptural, when he declared himself in this respect still a Pharisee after he had been converted to Christ for many years. Eternal judgment, too, is part of the former revelation. "God shall bring every work into judgment, with every secret thing, whether it be good, or whether it be evil" (Eccl. 12:14). Now let us note the contrast between these six items and the outstanding truths of Christianity. In the later revelation we have:

1. Repentance toward God (Acts 20:21).

2. Faith in our Lord Jesus Christ (Acts 20:21).

3. The cleansing of the conscience from dead works to serve

the living and true God by the washing of regeneration and renewing of the Holy Spirit.

4. The one offering of our Lord Jesus Christ with which every believer is fully identified.

5. The out-resurrection from among the dead (Phil. 3:11).

6. No judgment for the believer in Christ.

Note how vividly the contrast is developed in the New Testament.

The believer not only repents from dead works, but there is a complete change of attitude toward God. Faith is now in the Lord Jesus Christ definitely set forth as the sinner's only Savior. No outward cleansing will suffice; no washings with literal water or sprinkling of the blood of animal sacrifices, but cleansing from every sin by the precious blood of the Lord Jesus Christ and the washing of water by the Word applied in the Spirit's power. In place of the laying on of hands upon often-repeated sacrifices, the believer can now say in the words of the well-known hymn:

> My faith would lay her hand
> On that blest head of Thine;
> While like a penitent I stand,
> And there confess my sin.
>
> My soul looks back to see
> The burden Thou didst bear,
> When hanging on th' accursed tree,
> And knows her guilt was there.
>
> —Isaac Watts

Then we have today the blessed unfolding of the truth that there are two resurrections; not as some put it, a general resurrection of the dead at the last day, but the resurrection from among the dead at the coming of our Lord Jesus Christ for all His own. And as to judgment we now know, or at least we should know, that the believer shall not come into judgment but has already passed out of death into life. It is, then, to this full unfolding of New Testament truth that these Hebrew believers are called to "go on." This is Christianity, and Christianity is here designated as "perfection," distinguishing it from the imperfect or partial revelation of former days.

This, then, clears the way for the perplexing passage in verses 4–8. There were many Hebrews who in the beginning professed to acknowledge the messiahship of Jesus and were eyewitnesses of the marvelous things that took place at Pentecost and afterward. But as the Lord did not return and the promised kingdom was not immediately established, it was easy to understand how many of these, if lacking personal faith in Christ as Savior, would eventually give up the messianic confession and go back to Judaism which they knew to be a divinely revealed religion. This was a very serious thing, and yet it was something to which all these Hebrews would be exposed if they did not make a clean break with Judaism and go on to the perfection of Christianity. As to those who had already apostatized, it was too late to help them. They had made their choice and acted accordingly; and having experienced so much that was new and wonderful and then turned away from it all, they would be the hardest people on earth to change again. It is impossible, we are told, to renew again to repentance those once enlightened. It is important to notice that the word "renew" does not imply, as J. N. Darby has pointed out, a renewal or change, but to make what is entirely new. This could never be true again of those who had given up their Christian profession. It is not a definite statement that there is no possible hope for the recovery of such, but it is a declaration that they could never now come into all the blessing of Christianity as a new thing. They had already tried it out, they would tell you, and had deliberately given it up. Such must be left with God, whereas those who really valued the truth were urged to press on to fuller knowledge.

Some object to the thought that anyone could go as far as these apostates had gone without being regenerated, but verse 9 is proof positive that such is the case. Notice the five things that are stated of these who had turned back:

1. They had been at one time enlightened as to the claims of Jesus the Messiah.

2. They had tasted the sweetness of the heavenly gift, but this does not in itself imply that they had eaten of the Living Bread.

3. They were made partakers of Holy Spirit. The definite article is purposely omitted in the original. It was not that the Holy Spirit as a divine person had ever indwelt them, but they had participated in the blessing that the Spirit had given.

4. They had tasted the good Word of God, having listened to the good news of the gospel and to a certain extent appreciated the message that it brought.

5. They had been eyewitnesses of the works of power of the coming age, as were all who beheld the mighty miracles wrought by our Lord and His apostles.

Now as we consider each one of these items separately it will, I think, become clearly manifest that all might be true of persons who had never experienced the regenerating grace of the Spirit of God.

Everyone who listens to the message of the new dispensation is thereby enlightened, for "the darkness is past, and the true light now shineth" (1 John 2:8), and that Light illuminates all who come under its gracious influence. But, alas, men may refuse the Light and, by turning away from it, go back into darkness. How many there are who have been deeply stirred as they heard of the Gift of God's Son from heaven and yet have never, like the Samaritan woman, judged themselves in the presence of the Lord and truly eaten this Sacred Food. To be a "partaker of Holy Spirit" is not at all the same thing as to be born of the Spirit, sealed by the Spirit, indwelt by the Spirit, anointed by the Spirit, baptized by the Spirit into the body of Christ, or filled with the Holy Spirit. It is simply to be made aware of the mighty power of the Spirit working upon the hearts and minds of men bringing conviction, and wooing the heart toward Christ. One might tremble under this supernatural power and yet turn away from the message of the Spirit which if truly believed would bring life and peace. Many, too, who have listened eagerly to the Gospel, the good Word of God, and have recognized to a certain extent the preciousness of the message, have failed to eat the Word. Jesus did not say, "He that tasteth of me shall live by me"; but, "He that eateth me shall live by me." It is a definite act of faith which becomes a habit of life. Then it is important to notice that the powers of the coming age (not the world to come, merely) are the works that will characterize the return of our Lord and the millennial kingdom; in other words, miracles which were given as a sign to the Jews in order to authenticate the ministry of our Lord and His apostles. We read in John of many who believed on Him when they saw the signs that He did, yet who went back and walked no more with Him. And so it seems clear that these apostates were persons who had an outward acquaintance with Christianity but never knew what it was to receive the Lord Jesus as their own personal Savior. Definitely authenticated by works of power as He was, they still turned away from Him, and in so doing crucified for themselves the Son of God afresh, making a show of Him. This would be true of all who turned back from Christianity to Judaism.

In the two verses that follow, the apostle uses a parable to make clear what is in his mind. He depicts two pieces of ground; both have been cultivated in the same way; both are warmed by the same sun; both drink in their share of the same rain; but one produces useful herbs for those for whose sakes it has been tilled, thus partaking of blessing from God. The other brings forth only the fruit of the curse, thorns and briars; it is worthless, and in danger of being completely given up when its good-for-nothing fruit is burned. What is the difference between these two pieces of ground? In the one case, you have good soil into which has fallen good seed. In the other, there is barren soil and the good seed has not been fruitful. The lesson is plain. Here are two Jews, let us say, who have been brought up side by side. Both have been interested in the law of Moses and the teachings of the prophets. Both have entertained the messianic hope. Both have listened to the preaching of devoted servants of Christ. Both have become deeply interested in the Gospel. Both have been astounded at the mighty signs following the proclamation of the new message. Both make a profession of Christianity. Both are baptized and take their places in the Christian company. One of them bears the fruit of the Spirit in his life and becomes a devoted follower of the Savior. The other manifests no evidence of new life at all, and eventually repudiates Christianity and goes back to Judaism. He is not actually cursed as yet, for in the mercy of God he may eventually realize his fearful sin, but it is most unlikely. He has made his choice, and is therefore nigh unto cursing. Now what is the difference between these two men? The one has truly turned to God in repentance, and the incorruptible seed of the Gospel has fallen into the prepared soil of an honest upright heart. The other has become intellectually acquainted with and interested in Christianity, but the good seed has fallen upon an unrepentant heart and has borne no fruit.

That we have not been mistaken in applying the passage in this way is definitely settled by the statement of verse 9. The apostle says, "But, beloved, we are persuaded better things [concerning] you, and things that accompany salvation, though we thus speak." They needed the warning and the urge to go on, but he was assured that those to whom he was addressing himself were truly saved people. If he saw in them better things than he had already referred to in verses 4–5, it is evident that one might have the experience of the privileges there enumerated and not have salvation.

The proof of their reality was seen in their faithful service and love to fellow-saints leading to self-denying ministry. This gracious spirit he desires them to show to the end in the full assurance of hope, not giving way to slothfulness, but imitating those in past ages who, through faith and patience, became inheritors of the promise. He instances the case of their father Abraham to whom God swore by himself, "Surely blessing I will bless thee, and multiplying I will multiply thee," but to whom the promise was fulfilled only after long waiting. The word and oath of God were all that Abraham had for many years, but he held on in faith because he knew that God could not be untrue to His promise. And so we too have strong encouragement to press on counting upon God—we who, like the manslayer of old, have fled for refuge to lay hold on the hope set before us; that is, the hope of final and eternal salvation through our Lord Jesus Christ. This hope is to us the soul's anchor, not cast into the hold of the ship, that is, dependent upon our own frames and experiences, nor resting upon the shifting sands of human systems of thought; but fastened to the propitiatory, the mercy seat, inside the veil. This anchor has been carried in by Jesus our Forerunner. So that though we be here on earth tossed about upon the sea of time, "our anchor holds within the veil." It has been pointed out by others that the word translated "forerunner" was a nautical term used to designate a small boat. The mouths of many of the Greek harbors were not passable at low tide by ships of heavy draught on account of the sand bars, and so it was customary to place the anchor in the forerunner and, rowing over the bar, to cast it in the harbor, thus securing the ship until the tide should rise. The figure is readily applied to the soul's relation to our ascended Lord, who now ministers in the Holiest on our behalf, a High Priest according to the order of Melchisedek. He has entered into the very presence of God as our Representative, and His presence there is the pledge that we shall soon follow.

The Melchisedek Priesthood Superior to That of Aaron (Heb. 7)

We have seen how in 5:5–10 the apostle began to speak of the Melchisedek priesthood of Christ. But from 5:11–6:20 he turned aside into a lengthy parenthesis in order to prepare his readers for a better understanding of this important subject. In our present chapter he develops it fully. In the first three verses he dwells upon Melchisedek himself, and incidentally gives a wonderful key to the interpretation of the types found in the Old Testament and also a remarkable confirmation of the doctrine of verbal inspiration.

There is no reason to think of Melchisedek as in himself a mysterious personage, possibly supernatural, or even as some have supposed a pre-incarnate appearance of our Lord Jesus Christ. If any ask, "Who is Melchisedek?" the only proper answer is "Melchisedek." He was not Shem the son of Noah, nor Job of the land of Uz, nor Cheops the builder of the great pyramid, as some have endeavored to prove. He was, as is distinctly stated, Melchisedek, King of Salem. All that we know of him is given us in Genesis 14:18–20. This historical account depicts him as a royal priest reigning in Salem, the city that was afterward known as Jerusalem. Long before the Levitical economy had been established and a special family set apart for the priesthood he, like Job and Abraham, offered sacrifices as a priest of the Most High God. In the divine providence he met Abraham and his triumphant band as they returned from defeating Chedorlaomer and his allies. It is noticeable that the King of Sodom was on his way to meet Abraham when the latter was intercepted by Melchisedek, who came to bless him in the name of the Most High God, and whose spiritual authority Abraham recognized by giving him tithes of all the spoils. Strengthened by the bread and wine administered by Salem's king-priest, Abraham was prepared to refuse the alluring gifts of the King of Sodom, representative of the world in all its impurity and debasement.

In Psalm 110 our Lord is prophetically saluted as a Priest forever after the order of Melchisedek. He is to come forth from the new Jerusalem after the Armageddon conflict as a royal Priest to bless His delivered people in that day of His power.

Now observe how remarkably the Spirit of God sets His seal upon the verbal inspiration of the Old Testament. Our attention is drawn to the fact that this royal hierarch is first by interpretation King of Righteousness, and after that also King of Salem, which is, King of Peace. If the order of the names had been reversed, God's beautiful type would have been spoiled, but standing just as they do, the names Melchisedek and Salem are in perfect agreement with truth elsewhere revealed. Righteousness must come before peace. We are told in Isaiah 32:17, "The work of righteousness shall be peace; and the effect of righteousness quietness and assurance for ever." And so in the great gospel epistle to the Romans we first learn how the righteousness of God has been maintained in the cross before we are told of peace with God which is ours by faith. So exact is Scripture that the changing of the order of the original words would throw all into confusion.

Verse 3 has perplexed many, but it simply declares that so far as Scripture is concerned, Melchisedek appears upon its sacred page "without father, without mother, without descent [or genealogy], having neither beginning of days, nor end of life; but made like unto the Son of God; abideth a priest continually." That is, in the book of Genesis, in which we find so many genealogies, this man, in spite of his importance, has none. There is no record of his parentage, his birth, or his death. He simply appears for a moment, then vanishes from our sight, never even to be mentioned again in the Word of God until the prophecy of Psalm 110. Thus he is an apt type of our ever-living Savior and High Priest. Again let us worship as we contemplate the perfection of Scripture; just as perfect in what it omits as in what it relates!

In verses 4–10 we have the superiority of the Melchisedek priesthood over that of Levi brought out very clearly. Levi was not born until many years after the event mentioned in Genesis 14. Abraham, however, was the father of all the Hebrew race, and therefore all the twelve tribes—including of course Levi, from whom came the priestly family—were represented in him when he recognized the superiority of Melchisedek by paying tithes to him and received his high priestly blessing. Unquestionably, says the apostle, "the less is blessed of the better"; and so in this double way the surpassing greatness of this royal priest is emphasized. "Levi," we are told, "who received tithes, paid tithes in Abraham. For he was yet in the loins of his father, when Melchisedek met him." Just as the entire human race was on trial in Adam, so the Levitical priesthood was represented in the patriarch Abraham when he acknowledged the superiority of Melchisedek by his attitude toward him.

The ground is now clear to show how the Melchisedek priesthood of our Lord Jesus Christ surpasses in every way the Aaronic. It is evident that if perfection had come under the Levitical priesthood, in connection with which the law was given, there would have been no occasion for God to set it aside and raise up another Priest after a different and better order. Our Lord's priesthood, of course, was after the character of Aaron; that is, His person and work were typified by the high priest and his service in connection with the tabernacle. But He does not belong to that order. He is, as was Melchisedek, King and Priest by divine fiat, not by human succession. This involves a complete setting aside of the old covenant, for "the priesthood being changed, there is made of necessity a change also of the law." Israel stood or fell with the priesthood. If God accepted the high priest on the great day of atonement, for instance, it involved the acceptance of the nation. If the high priest was rejected then the people were set aside. No high priest was ever to rend his garments (Lev. 10:6). When Caiaphas in his excitement and indignation rent his clothes, the priesthood passed away from the house of Aaron. And with it went the entire legal economy which was superseded by the marvelous dispensation of the grace of God.

According to Levitical law, our Lord had no title to the priesthood at all. As to the flesh, He sprang from the tribe of Judah, not from that of Levi; but this does not in any way militate against His priesthood since it is of an altogether different order. He is consecrated, not in accordance with a legal enactment, but in all the might of resurrection "after the power of an endless life." As Priest forever after the order of Melchisedek, He has brought in a new and better regime than that of the law. And so the commandment going before has been set aside. It was weak and unprofitable in the sense that it could not accomplish that for which it was proposed; namely, to give man a righteous standing before God, inasmuch as the flesh or the carnal mind is not subject to the law of God, neither indeed can be. So it was useless as a ground for blessing. It made nothing perfect; therefore it had to give way to the introduction of a better hope by which we draw nigh to God. This better hope is founded upon the principle of grace of which Melchisedek is the exemplification. And so by divine oath Jesus has become the surety of a better covenant.

In verses 23–28 the contrast is between the dying priests of the old order and the ever living High Priest at God's right hand. There was a constant succession of priests in olden days, for death was continually taking its toll of them. But our Lord's priesthood is unchangeable because He continues "unto the ages," the strongest expression in the Greek language for eternity.

Thus as the ever-living One, He is able to deliver completely those who draw near to God by Him, seeing He ever lives to make intercession for them. It should be noted that salvation to the uttermost here does not simply mean salvation from every kind of sin, but is even greater than that—salvation forevermore. He whom God saves is saved eternally, for He who died for him lives to keep him and to complete the work He began. And thus our souls are stirred to worship and thanksgiving as we realize how suited our Great High Priest is to the need of those who were once unholy, harmful and defiled, sinful and degraded; for He gives us a perfect representation before the throne of God. He is everything that we were not and should have been. He is holy, harmless, undefiled, and separate from sinners and higher than the heavens, and He is all this for us. Nor is it necessary that He, like the high priests of old, should offer daily sacrifices. They offered for their own sins, for they were themselves unclean, and then they offered in behalf of the people. But these sacrifices never settled the sin question. He, by His one offering up of Himself upon the cross, has completed the work that saves, and settled the sin question for all eternity. The law constituted men high priests who were themselves infirm and unreliable, but the divine oath has proclaimed Jesus to be a Priest forever, He who is as to the mystery of His person, the Son of the Eternal Father.

What could the Spirit of God Himself say to make clearer the superiority of the priesthood of the new dispensation over that of the old? And with the priesthood, of course, is linked the entire sacrificial system. No Jew ever found settled peace or a purged conscience through recourse to the altar and the priest of the tabernacle or the temple. Undoubtedly wherever there was real faith, God met His people in grace, and by the Spirit gave them an inward sense of acceptance and joy in Himself, but this was not based upon the Levitical system. It was all in view of the eventual coming into the world of the Seed of the woman, who was to bruise the serpent's head and to be Himself wounded for His people's transgressions and bruised for their iniquities. The pious Israelite obeyed the commandment of the law and acted in accordance with the Mosaic ritual because God had so ordained for the time then present. Faith would lead him to do exactly as the Lord had said, but the ground of his peace rested not on the typical system but on that which it illustrated, the finished work of Christ. It was hard even for converted Hebrews to fully realize this, hence the care with which the Holy Spirit through the apostle takes up each detail in His effort to deliver them from Judaism and bring them out into the full light and liberty of Christianity.

In closing our study of this chapter, I would point out the distinction between the expression used here, "He offered up Himself," and that found in 9:14, where we read, "Christ, who through the eternal Spirit offered himself without spot to God." He "offered Himself" at His baptism in the Jordan, when the Holy Spirit descended upon Him, thus manifesting the Father's good pleasure and pointing Him out as the perfect sacrifice, who alone was able to fulfill all righteousness on behalf of guilty sinners. But it was at the cross that He actually "offered up Himself" when He voluntarily became the great sin offering. It is important to remember that the death of Jesus was not merely man's answer to the grace of God as seen in Christ. None could have put Him to death had He not of His own volition yielded up His life. He Himself declared, "No man taketh [my life] from me, but I lay it down of myself. I have power to lay it down, and I have power to take it again. This commandment have I received of my Father" (John 10:18). In the fullest possible sense He laid down that life voluntarily when He allowed wicked men to nail Him to that cross. There He took the sinner's place and bore the sinner's judgment. We speak of this as the finished work of Christ. But when we think of His High priesthood we are on other ground altogether. This is His unfinished work, the work that will never be completed as long as any of His redeemed are in the place of testing and in need of succor.

The Mediator of the New Covenant (Heb. 8)

The Ascended Priest (Heb. 8:1–6)

We now have a summing up of the instruction we have already received concerning the priesthood of our Blessed Lord. We see in Him a High Priest who through His own inherent right has taken a place which no Levitical priest could ever take. Instead of merely being permitted to enter once a year into the Holy of Holies, and that only for a few moments, not daring to sit down in the presence of God, our Lord Jesus Christ, as the ascended Man, has entered into the heavenly sanctuary and is there seated on the right hand of the throne of the Majesty in the heavens. There He ministers in the

Holiest in that glorious tabernacle of which the earthly tent was but a type.

How important it is for us to realize that we are represented before God by a Man in the glory, for though we no longer know Christ after the flesh, yet He has gone up to heaven as the representative Man to appear in the presence of God on our behalf.

The earthly high priest of old was appointed to offer both gifts and sacrifices. By gifts we understand those offerings which were the expression of the grateful, adoring hearts of the people of Israel. The sacrifices, on the other hand, had to do directly with making expiation for sin. Our Lord did this latter when He offered Himself up on the cross. But now that He is ministering in the heavenly sanctuary, it is of course necessary that He have something to offer. He presents before God our prayers and praises. Our heartfelt worship ascends to the Father by Him.

> Our great High Priest is sitting
> At God's right hand above;
> For us His hands uplifted
> In sympathy and love.
> —Lord Adalbert Percy Cecil

> To all our prayers and praises,
> Christ adds His sweet perfume,
> And love the censer raises,
> These odours to consume.
> —Mary Bowley

We may often be discouraged as we realize something of the imperfections even of our highest and best efforts to glorify God. Like William Cowper, we may exclaim:

> Sin twines itself about my thoughts,
> And slides into my prayers.

But it is blessed to know that nothing reaches God that is not perfect. Our Great High Priest takes out of our prayers and praises everything that is unholy or of the flesh, everything that is contrary to the nature of the God we adore. Then to what is left, He adds His own infinite perfections and thus presents all to the Father on our behalf.

His priesthood is altogether heavenly in character, for, "If he were on earth he should not be a priest, seeing that there are priests that offer gifts according to the law: who serve unto the example and shadow of heavenly things." This is not to say that He never acted in a priestly capacity while in this scene. He certainly did. As a Priest, He prayed for His disciples. In the seventeenth of John we have a wonderful sample of His High Priestly intercession. As Priest too, He offered Himself upon the cross as the supreme sacrifice for sin, as in the case of Aaron offering the bullock and the goat on the great day of atonement. But the point is, His entire priesthood was heavenly in character. It was not inherited after the Aaronic order. Looked at from that standpoint, He would not be a Priest at all, as He did not belong to the tribe of Levi or the household of Aaron. He is the Second Man, the Lord from heaven, and as such He is our Great High Priest, fulfilling the types and shadows of heavenly things, as set forth, for instance, in the book of Leviticus. In fact everything in connection with the tabernacle and its service was typical of Christ, picturing His glorious person and His wondrous work. This was why God was so particular in regard to all its details. "Moses was admonished of God," we are told, "when he was about to make the tabernacle: See, saith he, that thou make all things according to the pattern showed to thee in the mount." There was no room for human ingenuity or for Moses' own thoughts. All must be as ordered of God, for He alone knew the Son and the work He was to accomplish.

And now that the typical dispensation has been replaced by the present economy of grace, Christ has entered upon His better ministry, owing to the fact that He is the Mediator of a better covenant which was established upon better promises. The covenant of old depended upon man's ability to carry out its requirements. God in effect said, "If you will do thus and so, I will do certain things." Thus the promise of blessing rested upon man's ability to claim that blessing on the ground of his obedience to the law. No man ever could obtain the promises on that basis. And so our Lord Jesus took upon Himself the curse of a broken law, was made a curse for us, became the great sin offering, and now has become the Mediator of a better covenant, in which all the promise is on God's part and man receives every blessing as pure grace.

The Better Covenant Supersedes the Old (Heb. 8:7–13)

Had that first covenant been perfect, it would never have been set to one side and a new covenant brought in. But because of its imperfection on account of the weakness and frailty of the flesh, God had declared long before the coming of our Lord Jesus Christ into the world that a new covenant was to be consummated with Israel and Judah. The apostle quotes from Jeremiah 31:31–34:

> For finding fault with them, he saith, Behold, the days come, saith the Lord, when I will make a new covenant with the house of Israel and the house of Judah: not according to the covenant that I made with their fathers in the day when I took them by the hand to lead them out of the land of Egypt; because they continued not in my covenant, and I regarded them not, saith the Lord. For this is the covenant that I will make with the house of Israel after those days, saith the Lord; I will put my laws into their mind, and write them in their hearts: and I will be to them a God, and they shall be to me a people: and they shall not teach every man his neighbour, and every man his brother, saying, Know the Lord: for all shall know me, from the least to the greatest. For I will be merciful to their unrighteousness, and their sins and their iniquities will I remember no more. (Heb. 8:8–12)

This new covenant is clearly a reaffirmation of the unconditional covenant made with Abraham, which the law, coming in centuries later, could not annul. During all the present years of wandering Israel and Judah are under the curse of that broken law. But in the regeneration, when they shall be gathered back to their own land and restored to the favor of the Lord, this covenant of grace will be made with them.

It is most important to realize that nowhere are we told of a covenant made with the church. In Romans 9:4 we learn that "the covenants" pertained to Israel. They were the chosen people with whom the Sinaitic covenant was made. According to the terms of that covenant they have forfeited all claim upon God's favor. But He cannot deny Himself. He can never go back upon the covenant made with Abraham, by the terms of which He promised blessing unconditionally to Abraham's seed. These promises He reiterates in the new covenant. The blood of that covenant has been shed upon the cross. Our Lord said, as He gave the communion cup to His disciples, "This is the new covenant in My blood which is shed for you." On the basis of that precious blood all who now believe in Him who shed it, enter into the spiritual blessings of the new covenant, even though Gentiles after the flesh, and therefore by nature, "strangers to the covenants of promise." But in the fullness of time, when the day of Israel's blessing shall arrive, the new covenant will be confirmed to them and they will be born of God—"a nation shall be born in a day"—and He will own them as His covenant people. His laws will then be instilled in their minds and written upon their hearts, and they will render to Him glad, happy service, not in order to make themselves worthy of covenant blessing, but because of the gladness of their souls when they know Him as their God and realize that they are indeed His ransomed people. The day of their blindness will have gone forever. The veil will be taken away from their hearts. No longer in need of human instruction, they shall all know the Lord from the least to the greatest in that wondrous day when He will be merciful to their unrighteousness and will remember their sins and iniquities no more.

While this does not reach the full height of Christian blessing, yet it will be wonderful grace indeed shown to the people who failed so terribly when they crucified the Lord of glory. The new covenant says nothing of entrance into the Holiest, as we now know it; nothing of being raised up together and seated together in Christ Jesus in the heavenlies; nothing of union with Him as members of His body by the indwelling Holy Spirit. It is blessing for the earth and on the earth in the coming day. But the fact that all these heavenly privileges are secured for the church now by the shedding of the same blood of the covenant that is to procure future blessing for Israel, leads the apostle in the chapters that follow to stress our present title to enter into the Holiest, while Israel and Judah are still dispersed among the Gentiles, waiting for the day when the new covenant will be confirmed to them.

The very expression "a new covenant," in itself makes the former testament null and void. It served its purpose up to the cross. Now that "which decayeth and waxeth old is ready to vanish away." It is pathetic how little many Christians enter into this and understand how the sacrifice of our Lord Jesus Christ has freed us from all obligation to that temporary dispensation. It is to be feared that many who sometimes sing of such liberty fail really to understand its import.

> Free from the law! Oh, happy condition!
> Jesus hath bled, and there is remission;
> Cursed by the law and bruised by the fall,
> Christ hath redeemed us once for all.
>
> —Philip P. Bliss

Not yet do the earthly people understand this, and many who in a vague way have trusted in Christ and are undoubtedly regenerated, are still far from enjoying the liberty that is ours in Christ. Our present relationship to God is one of pure grace during this parenthetical period, in which God, having set aside Israel after the flesh, is taking out from among the Gentiles a people for His name. After this work is completed, He will build again the tabernacle of David that is fallen down and will make a new covenant with those in Israel and Judah who will turn to the Lord in that day.

The important thing to see is that the new covenant, as such, does not go beyond blessing on the earth. It has to do with the earthly side of the kingdom of God, to enter into which new birth is a prerequisite, as our Lord told Nicodemus. This is what is meant by the writing of the divine law upon the hearts in the day that Israel and Judah will turn to the One who was once rejected.

The Perfection of Christ's Work (Heb. 9–10)

The Earthly Sanctuary a Shadow of the Heavenly (Heb. 9:1–10)

As we enter now into the very heart of this precious portion of God's Word, the apostle at the outset directs our attention to the typical character of the sanctuary and its service under the former dispensation. It will be noted throughout that he has the tabernacle in view rather than the temple. This is not, as some have supposed, because the construction of the temple was any less divinely ordered than that of the tabernacle. David plainly declared to Solomon, in giving him the plan of the more permanent sanctuary, "All this, . . . the LORD made me understand in writing by his hand upon me, even all the works of this pattern" (1 Chron. 28:19). But the temple types evidently prefigure millennial glory and blessing and will be fully entered into and understood in that day of Jehovah's power. The tabernacle, on the other hand, which was a temporary dwelling place picturing truth for a pilgrim people, has its application to the present times when the Holy Spirit, typified by the cloudy pillar of old, is leading the new dispensation company through the wilderness of this world, on to the rest that remains for the people of God.

As the first covenant was but for a time, so with the first tabernacle. It had ordinances of divine service and a worldly sanctuary. By "worldly" we are not to understand "unspiritual," but rather that which is in contrast with the heavenly.

The tabernacle itself was, as we well know, divided into two parts, the first called the Holy Place, and the second, the Holiest of all, separated by the sacred veil. And as the apostle points out the various pieces of furniture connected with each compartment, we have another most striking illustration of the absolute verbal inspiration of the Holy Scriptures; and this, in regard to a point which unbelievers have eagerly seized upon, claiming that it showed the very opposite, namely, apparent inaccuracy on the part of the sacred writer.

When he speaks of the first compartment, he says, "*Wherein* was the candlestick and the table, and the showbread." He makes no mention of the golden altar of incense. Had he forgotten that this altar stood immediately before the veil? Or was there some divine reason for omitting mention of it in this connection?

All becomes very clear when we carefully note the next three verses: "And after the second veil, the tabernacle which is called the Holiest of all; *which had* the golden censer, and the ark of the covenant overlaid round about with gold, wherein was the golden pot that had manna, and Aaron's rod that budded, and the tables of the covenant; and over it the cherubims of glory shadowing the mercyseat; of which we cannot now speak particularly" (vv. 3–5). Now observe carefully the change from the expression "wherein" to the altogether different term "which had." And then notice that the golden censer is really the golden incense altar. The original is *thumiasterion*, which is the ordinary word for an incense altar. It is not at all the same as the word used in Revelation 8:3, 5 for a censer. This is *libanotos*.

Any ordinary reader of English can see how utterly different the two words are. There can be no question, then, but that "censer" here means the incense altar. But why did the writer not say it was in the Holy Place? Why does he plainly connect it with the Holiest?

The answer is perfectly simple. It belonged to the Holiest because it typified Christ's person and intercessory work in the Holiest of all. But during all the Old Testament dispensation it must stand outside the veil where it could be approached by the priests, and yet so near the veil that the moment this curtain was rent in twain from the top to the bottom the fragrant smoke of the incense entered the Holiest. The apostle does not say it was in the Holiest, but he does declare it belonged to the Holiest "which had the golden incense altar." So then the apparent imperfection is really a most beautiful evidence of the perfection of Holy Writ.

As long as the old dispensation lasted the priests had no access into the Holiest. They went only into the first tabernacle and accomplished the liturgical service. Once a year the high priest alone was permitted to enter the sacred inner chamber where the Shechinah hovered over the mercy seat. Nor could he approach without atoning blood, which he offered first of all for himself as being but a sinful man, and also for the failures of the people.

By this arrangement, the Holy Spirit was declaring the solemn fact that the way into the immediate presence of God had not yet been made known, nor could be, so long as that first tabernacle had any standing before Him. The expression "was yet standing" is misleading. It would suggest that the way into the Holiest was not made known until the destruction of the temple about A.D. 70, and thus many have understood it. But it clearly means that the way into the Holiest was not opened up so long as God recognized the first tabernacle. The moment Christ Jesus died upon the cross the entire typical system ceased to have any standing before God. It was but a figure for a time then present, and the gifts and sacrifices offered in connection with it were simply picturing the offering up of the body of our Lord Jesus Christ upon the cross. In themselves, they were of no real value. They could not settle the sin question, and therefore could not perfect the consciences of those who brought them. The many ordinances in connection with meats and drinks and different baptisms, whether of persons or things, in fact all the fleshly observances which were connected with the first covenant, were only intended to serve a temporary purpose and to be in force until the time of reformation; that is, until Christ by His death and resurrection fulfilled them all and brought in the present new and glorious dispensation of the grace of God.

The Superiority of the Sacrifice of Christ to All Those Offered Under the Old Dispensation (Heb. 9:11–23)

The apostle now proceeds to show how marvelously the one offering of our Lord Jesus Christ transcends all the types and shadows of old. He is both High Priest and Victim. As High Priest of good things to come, whose ministry is linked with a greater and more perfect tabernacle, that is, with the eternal dwelling place of God, He has by the presentation of His blood entered in once for all into the Holiest on the basis of an accomplished redemption. His work abides eternally before God. No failure on the part of His redeemed can touch the value of His finished work. Of old, every time an Israelite sinned he needed a new sacrifice; but Christ's one perfect offering up of Himself has settled the sin question for ever, and therefore no wandering of heart nor failure in life on the part of those who have availed themselves by faith of His atoning work can alter for one moment their standing before the throne of God.

> That which can shake the cross
> Can shake the peace it gave;
> Which tells me Christ has never died,
> Nor ever left the grave.

Because of the infinite value of His precious blood, He has fully met all the claims of divine justice and thus secured eternal redemption. The moment His blood was shed upon the cross its efficacy was recognized in heaven, thus answering to the sprinkling of the blood upon the mercy seat. But it is not only seen as sprinkled upon the throne of God but also upon the believer, who is thus purged from all uncleanness.

Verse 13 brings vividly before us the ordinance of the red heifer as given in Numbers 19. The heifer was burned to ashes, the ashes mixed with water, and this water of separation was sprinkled upon an unclean Israelite in order to make him fit for participation in the service of the earthly sanctuary. Ashes in this connection became eloquent indeed. They cried aloud, as did the expiring Savior, "It is finished!" For ashes tell of fire burned out never to burn again. And so the failing believer has daily recourse to the washing of water by the Word, bringing afresh to his soul the truth of that finished work wherein every sin was settled for when Jesus died upon the tree. Therefore the apostle says, "How much more shall the blood of Christ, who through the Eternal Spirit offered Himself without spot to God, purge your conscience from dead works to serve the living God?" He, the Sinless One, offered Himself to take the sinner's place, and this in the power of the Eternal Spirit; and through the shedding of His blood our consciences are purged from works of death and we are set free to serve the living God. The Israelite of old who was defiled by coming in contact with the dead, had recourse to the water of separation. But all our best efforts were defiled by the fact that we ourselves in our unsaved state were dead in trespasses and in sins. Now, with all the past settled for, we are free to serve the living God in faith and in the power of a new life.

Christ is therefore the Mediator of the new covenant, which is founded upon His own death, whereby He settled for the transgressions of all who turned to God in faith during the times of the first covenant, that they, with us, might receive the promise of the eternal inheritance. This is undoubtedly the meaning of the expression, "The redemption of the transgressions that were under the first covenant." The sins of Old Testament saints were not actually put away until Christ accomplished redemption on the cross. Then these came into all the blessing of the new covenant which He sealed with His own blood.

There has been much controversy as to whether the change from covenant to testament, in the sense of a will, is intended in the verses that follow. But the two are so intimately connected that there would seem to be no reason for difficulty in understanding the truth presented. The old covenant was God's will for His people prior to the coming of Christ and was sealed by the blood of calves and goats, which Moses sprinkled upon the book and all the people saying, "This is the blood of the testament which God hath enjoined unto you." The new covenant is the will of our blessed Lord whereby He decrees that all who put their trust in Him should receive part in that eternal inheritance which He gladly shares with all believers. By His death this testament came into force. Apart from His death, there could be no such blessing for guilty sinners. A testament is in effect after men are dead. His death upon the cross puts this new covenant, or testament, or will, into operation, and inasmuch as it is a covenant of pure grace, all who believe enter into the good of it even before the day when it is to be openly confirmed with Israel and Judah, as we saw in the previous chapter. The blood of the covenant having already been shed, there is nothing to hinder the outflow of blessing. The sprinkling of the blood under the old dispensation confirmed that covenant, and was a warning to the people that death would result for its violation; while at the same time it typified the shedding of the blood of the new covenant Victim. Therefore we are told that Moses sprinkled with blood both the tabernacle and all the vessels of the ministry, and "almost all things are by the law purged with blood; and without the shedding of blood there is no remission." This last statement is absolute. It is not restricted to the old covenant, as the verses that immediately follow make plain. It was necessary in the plan of God that the patterns and figures of things in the heavens should be purified with the blood of animal sacrifices, but the realities with better things than those of old. The heavenly things need purification because sin began in the heavens. It was there that Satan fell, and thus the heavens became unclean. Christ's sacrifice is the basis for the purification of the polluted heavens and guarantees the bringing in of a new heaven and a new earth wherein dwells righteousness. Thus eventually, all in heaven and all on earth will be reconciled to God through the blood of the cross.

This, of course, is not Universalism. It does not imply the salvation of all who have lived on earth, and certainly not of fallen angels who defiled the heavens. But it does speak of a time coming when sin and sinners will be banished from the earth and the heavens, and God be all in all.

The Way into the Holiest Through the Blood of Jesus: His Entrance the Pledge of Ours (Heb. 9:24–10:22)

The ground has now been laid that enables the apostle to open up for us the special truth of the new dispensation, and to show how fully Christ has superseded all the types of old. In verses 24–28 of this ninth chapter we have what someone has very aptly designated, "the three appearings of our Lord Jesus Christ": He hath appeared, He doth appear, He shall appear. The order, however, is somewhat different, for the Holy Spirit dwells first on His present appearance as our Intercessor above, then turns our minds back to the time when He appeared to settle the sin question, and in the closing verses carries us forward to the glad hour when He shall appear the second time for our complete and glorious redemption.

In verse 24, then, we look by faith into the true tabernacle which is above, the Holy Places not made with hands, and there we see our blessed risen Lord as He appears in the presence of God on our behalf. He is there to give us a perfect representation before the throne of God and we are accepted in Him. He is also there to make intercession for us in view of human frailty and tendency to err. And as the apostle John shows us, He is there as our Advocate with the Father, to undertake for us when actual failure has come in and broken communion. How full and complete is His present service as He officiates for us in the Holy Places! We often speak, and rightly so, of the finished work of Christ. This refers of course to His vicarious atonement which took place upon the cross. But it is just as scriptural to speak of His unfinished work, if we have in mind this special ministry of intercession which He has been carrying on in the Holiest ever since He was received up in glory, and which will never be finished so long as one needy saint is in the place of testing here on earth. His Cross work can never be repeated. No repetition is required, for He settled the sin question perfectly when He took our place in judgment. And in this we have the great distinction between the legal sacrifices and His one offering of Himself, when in the consummation of the ages He appeared to put away sin by His mighty sacrifice. The offerings of old had to be repeated again and again because they did not possess value sufficient to settle the sin question. But His precious blood poured forth for our redemption was of such infinite value that it is sacrilegious even to think of adding to it in any way. Having officiated at the altar, answering to the type of the great Day of Atonement, He has now gone into the sanctuary in the value of His own blood, and by and by He will come out to bless His people as did the priest of old.

> And though a while He be
> Hid from the eyes of men,
> His people look to see
> Their Great High Priest again.
> —Thomas Kelly

Just as truly as men were under sentence of death with judgment beyond it, so Christ took that sentence upon Himself and was once offered to bear the sins of many. And just as certainly shall He appear unto them that look for Him the second time, altogether apart from the sin question, unto the complete and final salvation of all His own. Meantime the Holy Spirit has come forth to bear witness to the efficacy of His propitiatory work, while He Himself continues His ministry in the heavenly sanctuary.

It ought to be clear that the latter part of verse 28 is not intended to teach that only those who have advanced in knowledge along prophetical lines, and therefore live in daily expectation of the second coming of the Savior, shall be caught up to meet Him at His return. This is not at all what was in the mind of the writer, and is certainly not the teaching of the Holy Spirit elsewhere in Scripture. But just as all Israel could be said to look for the coming forth of the high priest who had sprinkled the mercy seat with the blood of atonement, so all believers look for the coming again of our Lord Jesus. There may not be much intelligence as to the mode of His coming, nor in regard to the order of events, but the renewed heart cries, "Come, Lord Jesus."

In the first eighteen verses of chapter 10 the contrast between the sacrifices under the law and His one offering is brought out more clearly than ever. It is important to follow the argument carefully and notice the close reasoning of the apostle as he contrasts the one with the other. The Levitical economy was but a shadow of the coming good things. It was not an exact delineation of these things. It was therefore impossible that the sacrifices offered upon Jewish altars yearly to perpetuity could perfect those who presented them so far as their consciences were concerned. For if the bringing of a lamb or a bullock could have settled the sin question, what necessity would there have been ever to repeat such a sacrifice? The worshippers, if actually once purged, would have been freed from all conscience of sins. Note carefully, he does not say *consciousness* of sins but *conscience* of sins. The distinction is most important. Today I may be conscious of sin in thought, word, and deed, but confessing my sins, I look up into the face of my Father with confidence, knowing that for these very sins the blood of Christ has answered, and thus my conscience is freed from condemnation. This could never be under the former order. Every sin called for a new offering, and then on the great Day of Atonement there was an annual sacrifice for all Israel. Notice verse 3: "In those sacrifices there is a remembrance again made of sins every year." Other translations have been suggested, all of which help to throw light on the meaning. The word translated "remembrance" might be rendered "recognition," "calling to mind," or "acknowledgment." But why such an acknowledgment of sins if the sacrifice could not actually purge them away? The figure of a promissory note might help here. Let us suppose one is in debt for a certain sum of money. He gives a note to run for a year. At the end of the year he finds himself unable to pay. He renews the note. The note has no real value in itself. Nor did the sacrifices have any moral or spiritual value in the sight of God. But in that note there is an acknowledgment of the debt from year to year. Now let us suppose someone who is well able to pay endorses the note, what then? When it becomes due, it is referred to him for settlement and he discharges the obligation.

The application is simple and clear. It was not possible that the blood of bulls and of goats should take away sins; but every time a believing Israelite brought his sacrifice to the altar, he was, so to speak, giving his note to God. He acknowledged his indebtedness, his sin, and accepted responsibility for the same. This was all he could do, but the pre-incarnate Christ endorsed every one of the notes and in the fullness of time came prepared to settle in full for all. "Wherefore when he cometh into the world, he saith, Sacrifice and offering thou wouldest not, but a body hast thou prepared me: in burnt offerings and sacrifices for sin thou hast had no pleasure. Then said I, Lo, I come (in the volume of the book it is written of me), to do thy will, O God" (vv. 5–7). Here indeed is the divine Endorser who undertakes in grace to meet every claim that the throne of God has against penitent sinners. In this passage, which is quoted from Psalm 40:6–8, it is interesting to observe that all four of the offerings of Leviticus 1–7 are in view. The word "sacrifice" refers to the peace offering. The term "offering" is really the *minchah*, that is, the "meal" offering. The other two terms are too clearly designated to need any explanation. All of them were of no avail to put away sin, and consequently it could be said of them that God had no pleasure in them. But when His own blessed Son came into the world to fulfill all these types, and to pay in His own person the redemption price, it is written: "It pleased the LORD to bruise him; he hath put him to grief: when thou shalt make his soul an offering for sin, he shall see his seed, he shall prolong his days, and the pleasure of the LORD shall prosper in his hand" (Isa. 53:10).

By the fulfillment of the declaration of Psalm 40 He actually wound up the old dispensation and brought in the new. "He taketh away the first, that he may establish the second."

When He said, "I come to do thy will," He spoke of course of the will of God in His coming to make expiation for inequity; and by His accomplishment of that will, we who believe in Him are now eternally set apart to God on the basis, not of our promises or feelings or of our personal righteousness, but of the offering of the body of Jesus Christ once for all. How slowly truths like these seem to seep into our souls and become part of our very beings. But one may safely say there is no lasting peace until this aspect of Christ's work has been laid hold of in faith.

Continuing, the writer reminds his readers that in the sanctuary of old the high priests were constantly ministering and carrying on a work which was never completed, because of the fact that those offerings could not take away sins. The expression "every priest standeth" is in itself significant. We do not read of a chair or a settee in the tabernacle or temple, for the priest's work was never done. But how different it is with our Great High Priest above! He, after having offered His one sacrifice for sins forever, sat down on the right hand of God, where He now waits until His enemies be made the footstool of His feet. Whether one connects the term *forever* with the expression "one sacrifice for sins" or with the sitting down, makes little difference. That sacrifice has eternal efficacy. On the other hand, as Priest-Victim, His work done, He sat down never to offer sacrifice again. His one offering is perfect and complete, and all who are linked with Him by faith appear before God in all the value of that finished work, perfected forever, because sanctified in Him.

Of this the Holy Spirit is a witness to us. He has come forth from the Father and the Son to bear testimony to the perfection of that finished work. And it is He who now opens up the Holy Scriptures of the Old Testament, giving us to see in them what saints of old never realized was there. Witness the quotation from Jeremiah 31:33–34. What was promised to Israel and Judah through the new covenant is now true of all who turn to Christ. By new birth God puts His laws in their hearts and writes them in their minds, and declares without any qualification, "Their sins and iniquities will I remember no more." This is complete justification from all things. No charge can now be brought against the one for whom Christ has settled everything. Therefore the blessed conclusion, "Where remission of these is, there is no more offering for sin" (v. 18).

This then entitles the "brethren" of Christ, the new priestly house, to enter with boldness as purged worshippers into the Holiest, the immediate presence of God, in all the infinite value of the blood of Jesus through that new and living way which He Himself opened for us when, by His death upon the cross, the veil was rent in twain, and God no longer was hidden, nor man in Christ shut out. So intimately are the redeemed and the Redeemer linked together, so truly are the High Priest and priestly house one before God, that we are urged to enter in spirit where He has gone, and to draw near to God with true hearts in the full assurance of that faith that is based upon the knowledge of an accomplished redemption; our hearts having been sprinkled by the blood of Christ from an evil conscience, and like the once-defiled Israelite, "our bodies having been washed with the water of purification." It is to be regretted that so few Christians seem to apprehend all this today. It is safe to say that for thousands who have hope in Christ, the veil might just as well never have been rent. They do not have any conception of liberty for access into the Holiest, but think of themselves as a people on probation still, who, if only faithful to their profession will eventually be fitted for admission into the presence of God. How much is thus lost through failure to understand the true Christian position which has been beautifully expressed in the words of an old hymn:

> Now we see in Christ's acceptance,
> But the measure of our own;
> He who lay beneath our sentence
> Seated high upon the throne.
> —George West Frazer

God sees every believer in Him, and the feeblest saint has title to immediate access into the Holiest through the atoning blood. The exhortation and warning that follow were never intended by the Holy Spirit to becloud this blessed truth in the slightest degree, but rather to accentuate the importance of holding fast what is here revealed.

Warning Against Apostasy; Evidences of Reality (Heb. 10:23–39)

After the gracious invitation to enter into the Holiest comes the counter exhortation of verses 23–25: "Let us hold fast the profession of our faith without wavering; (for he is faithful that promised); and let us consider one another to provoke unto love and to good works: not forsaking the assembling of ourselves together, as the manner of some is; but exhorting one another: and so much the more, as ye see the day approaching." In verse 23 *confession* would be a better word than *profession*, as in King James Version. We may profess what is not true. We confess that which is. The believer has declared his faith in a crucified, risen, and glorified Christ. He is exhorted to hold fast this great confession without turning either to the right or to the left, assured of the faithfulness of Him who gave the promises concerning His Son, and has in grace fulfilled them up to the present moment. One great promise remains to be confirmed at our Lord's return, and we may be assured that He who has never failed in one respect in regard to the past and present work of Christ, will be equally faithful in regard to that which is to come.

Three times we have the persuasive words, "let us." First, "Let us draw near" (v. 22); second, "Let us hold fast" (v. 23); and now, "Let us consider one another" (v. 24). The believer is not alone in his confession of Christ, nor is he to act in isolation. He is linked with others both by nature and grace, and he is called upon to seek to stir up his brethren unto love and to good works, assembling with fellow-saints for worship, prayer, and testimony, not coldly withdrawing himself as the manner of some, but remembering his responsibility toward his brethren is all the greater if some seem to have failed grievously and others are in danger of it. Nor is he to make special light on prophetic truth a reason for assuming a sectarian attitude toward his brethren. He needs them and they need him all the more as the day of Christ's glorious return to this earth approaches.

In verses 26–31 we have another side of things altogether. The warning, as in chapter 6, is against apostasy. We read:

> For if we sin wilfully after that we have received the knowledge of the truth, there remaineth no more sacrifice for sins, but a fearful looking for of judgment and fiery indignation, which shall devour the adversaries. He that despised Moses' law died without mercy under two or three witnesses: of how much sorer punishment, suppose ye, shall he be thought worthy, who hath trodden under foot the Son of God, and hath counted the blood of the covenant, wherewith he was sanctified, an unholy thing, and hath done despite unto the Spirit of grace? For we know him that hath said, Vengeance belongeth unto me, I will recompense, saith the Lord. And again, The Lord shall judge his people. It is a fearful thing to fall into the hands of the living God.

The warning here is based upon the perfection of the one sacrifice of Christ, which has been opened up in such a marvelous way in the preceding part of the chapter; as that of chapter 6 was based upon the manifest power of the Holy Spirit working in the Christian company, which was designed of God to exalt the person of Christ. To apostatize either from the truth as to His person or His finished work, means eternal ruin. It is not mere failure in the life that is here contemplated. The willful sin in this passage is the definite rejection of His atoning sacrifice. Nor is this simply the foolish and wicked determination of a moment, of which many have been guilty, but have afterward been brought to sincere repentance. The apostle really says, "If we *are sinning* wilfully after that we have received the knowledge of the truth, there remains no other sacrifice for sins." The verb is the present participle. It is what has become habitual. If, after fully examining what the Old Testament Scripture teaches concerning Christ and His work and comparing it with the New Testament presentation, thus having obtained the knowledge of the truth, one deliberately and persistently rejects it, God has nothing more to say to him. By so doing, he spurns the only means of salvation for Jew or Gentile. An apostate Hebrew might have reasoned within himself that the sacrifices still going on at the temple were all that he needed, and therefore, even though he had professed to be a follower of Christ, he would turn back to them; but this would be a fearful mistake. Those sacrifices no longer availed. Christ's atonement alone met the claims of God in respect to sin. And so the apostate had nothing to look forward to but the certainty of divine judgment and flaming wrath. Of old, the despiser of the first covenant died without mercy upon the testimony of two or three witnesses. But what was his guilt compared to that of the man who had become acquainted with the gospel message, had at one time been intellectually convinced of the truth, but for selfish reasons had finally turned away from it and gone back to Judaism? To do this was to tread under foot the Son of God and count the blood of the new covenant wherewith he was sanctified an unholy thing. Manifestly this could never be true of one born of God, for the Holy Spirit abiding within would preserve from so terrible a step. Yet what is the meaning of the expression, "The blood of the covenant wherewith he was sanctified?" The answer surely is that sanctification is here positional. Just as all Israel was set apart by the blood of the *old* covenant at Sinai, and yet any Israelite lacking faith could turn from all the privileges that were his by virtue of that blood, so today the entire professing church is set apart to God on earth in the value of the blood of the *new* covenant. But this does not preclude the possibility of abjuring this covenant sign and refusing the blessedness which it has purchased. The Holy Spirit delights to magnify Christ and to exalt His work. To refuse His testimony is to do despite unto the Spirit of grace. This expression, "the Spirit of grace," occurs only here in the New Testament, and is found only once in the Old Testament, and that in Zechariah 12:10.

There is a very interesting suggestion in verse 30 in corroboration of the position we have already taken as to the authorship of this epistle. We read, "We know him that hath said, Vengeance belongeth unto me, I will recompense, saith the Lord. And again, The Lord shall judge his people." These quotations are from Deuteronomy 32:35–36. The second one is an exact quotation from the Hebrew, but the first one is quoted neither from the Hebrew nor the LXX. It is the writer's own rendering of the passage, and is exactly the same in the Greek as the quotation in Romans 12:19. We know who the author of Romans was. We may be certain that the same hand penned the epistle to the Hebrews.

This word of warning closes for the moment with the solemn declaration, "It is a fearful thing to fall into the hands of the living God." All who reject the testimony He has given concerning His Son must meet Him in judgment; and we read elsewhere, "In thy sight shall no man living be justified" (Ps. 143:2). But "he who has died is justified from sin," as a literal rendering of Romans 6:7 tells us.

Satan has used the passage we have been considering to trouble and perplex honest souls whose sensitive consciences accuse them of failure to walk with God as they should. Such have often been made to fear that they were guilty of the willful sin here contemplated. But it is not the question of what is commonly called "backsliding" that is before us. Of this any real believer may often be guilty; but even when overwhelmed with failure, he clings more tenaciously than ever to the fact that Jesus is the only Savior and His sacrifice the only means of deliverance from sin's judgment. The apostate of this chapter has no such hope or consciousness. He has spurned utterly both the Christ and the cross. He holds the blood of Jesus in contempt, and hence for him there is nothing but doom ahead.

It is evident that from verse 32 to the end of the chapter, the writer is seeking to assure the hearts of all who have really trusted Christ that his words do not apply to them, while on the other hand he would warn them of the danger of turning their back in the slightest degree upon any truth that God had revealed. He bids them remember the former days, the days when upon first being awakened by the Holy Spirit and enlightened by the truth, they turned from the world for His dear sake and were content to suffer for His name, enduring a great fight of afflictions, sometimes suffering personally both by reproach and persecution, and at other times bearing the contempt of their former co-religionists because of fellowship with those who were suffering for Christ's sake. They had in this way manifested their love for him showing him every consideration possible after his imprisonment, even taking joyfully the spoiling of their goods, knowing on the authority of the Word of God that they had in heaven a better and enduring treasure. Having begun so well, and up to the present time continued in the part of devoted separation to Christ, he exhorts them so to continue to the end. "Cast not away therefore your confidence, which hath great recompense of reward. For ye have need of patience, that, after ye have done the will of God, ye might receive the promise" (vv. 35–36). Reward is distinguished from salvation. The latter is altogether by grace, and is ours from the moment we believe in the Lord Jesus Christ, but it is at His coming that we shall receive our reward. He says, "Behold, I come quickly, and my reward is with me, to give unto every man according as his work shall be." In view of this, how needful it is that we endure patiently, assured that when we have fulfilled the will of God concerning us, we shall receive in full the promised blessing at His return. "For yet a little while, and he that shall come will come, and will not tarry" (v. 37). This is a paraphrase of Habakkuk 2:3, which in the LXX reads, "For the vision is for a time, and it shall shoot forth at the end, and not in vain: though he should tarry, wait for him; for he will surely come and will not delay." It is Christ Himself who is before the eye of the prophet. He will fulfill every promise made to His suffering people when He returns in power and glory. Nor is His coming to be long delayed, though it may seem so sometimes to His waiting people. But we need to remember that "one day is with the Lord as a thousand years, and a thousand years as one day," so that not yet have two days gone by in God's reckoning since Jesus went away. Who knows that ere this second day is past He may be back again.

In the meantime God has said, "The just shall live by faith: but if any man draw back, my soul shall have no pleasure in him." This also is a quotation from Habakkuk 2:4. It is remarkable the way a brief text from an obscure Old Testament writer is used by the Spirit of God in emphasizing the great truth that is characteristic of the present age, "The just shall live by faith." We are justified by faith; we are maintained in a righteous life by faith; and by faith we live to God. If any, after making a profession such as this, turn back, they prove that there was no real faith in the soul, and God declares, He hath "no pleasure in them." But how comforting the words with which the chapter closes. What assurance they are designed to impart to every trusting one. "But we are not of them who draw back unto perdition; but of them that believe to the saving of the soul." There is an intellectual believing that saves no one. One may accept Christianity as a system one day and give it up the next. But he who truly trusts in Christ is saved even now, and will never draw back unto eternal loss. Concerning all such our Lord has said, "Those that thou gavest me, I have kept, and none of them is lost." And we are told that He who hath begun a good work in them will perform it unto the day of Christ. Therefore it should be plain that salvation is not in our keeping, but we ourselves are kept by the power of God. None can pluck us out of the hands of the Father and the Son. Eternal life would not be "eternal" if it were forfeitable and could ever be lost.

CHAPTER 4

The Path of Faith and the Heroes of Faith in All Dispensations

Hebrews 11

The Nature of Faith (Heb. 11:1–3)

Someone has called this eleventh chapter "God's honor roll." It is indeed a wonderful record of the triumphs of faith on the part of eminent servants of God in four different dispensations. Abel, Enoch, and Noah, in antediluvian days; Noah and Abraham himself in the dispensation of government; then Abraham, after the promise of the Seed, to Joseph the patriarch; and Moses and the other worthies of the dispensation of law. All these were but preparatory periods leading on to the present glorious dispensation of the grace of God. But in all these past ages we see that faith was the controlling power that enabled men to walk with God and triumph over the corrupting influences of their times. It is important to remember that God has never had two ways of saving men. While the revelation of His grace has come gradually, and various rites and ceremonies have been linked with it at different times, these latter have had nothing to do with regenerating or justifying the individual. It has always been true that faith in God's Word, whatever that Word may have been, has alone justified man before Him, and through that Word men have been saved in all ages, thus entering into His spiritual kingdom and recognizing His authority in a world at variance with that divine rule. This comes out very clearly in our present chapter. In verses 1–3 we are given to understand the nature of faith itself. "It is the substantiating of things hoped for, the conviction of things not seen," as Darby has translated it. That is, faith in what God has declared gives the soul absolute assurance and firm conviction of the reality of things which the natural eye has never seen. Yet these things are as real to the man of faith as anything that he can see, feel, taste, smell, or handle. In fact, they become even more real, for his senses might deceive him, but the Word of God he knows to be absolutely infallible. It was this positive realization that every word of God is true which quickened into newness of life believers in ancient times, and enabled them to bear testimony to things that the natural man could never apprehend by such evidence as appeals to his mind.

Men have speculated all through the centuries as to the origin of the universe, and have questioned whether matter is eternal, or whether it was directly created by God. But apart from revelation, no man can speak with certainty in regard to these things. Faith alone gives apprehension of the truth. By faith we understand that the worlds were made by the Word of God, so that the things which we now see were brought into existence at His command out of nothing. It is well known that the word translated "worlds" really means "ages," but the last part of the sentence shows that the material creation is in view; it is the material creation as passing through a series of changing ages, all of which were planned beforehand by God Himself, for the glory of His Son.

What a magnificent conception is this and how far beyond the highest thoughts of the mere natural scientist! Reverent, God-fearing men of science have always recognized the necessity of this divine revelation as to the origin of matter, and have had no difficulty with the sublime narrative of Genesis 1. It is only unbelief and willful rejection of the testimony of God that makes men stumble at and pervert so wondrous an unfolding of the beginnings of the created heavens and earth. Faith bows in subjection to the witness God has given and glorifies Him for such a marvelous unfolding of the divine wisdom. The late F. W. Grant has aptly pointed out the incongruity of the position of a scientist like Charles Darwin, whose great book, *The Origin of Species*, was hailed by many as throwing a flood of light upon the method of creation; and yet in that very book, Darwin never touches the question of origins! In the very nature of things, he cannot do so, for no man who is not subject to the Holy Spirit knows anything whatever about the beginnings of the material universe, and creatures living in it. But to faith all is plain. The simplest Christian with his Bible before him would say, "Through faith we understand."

Faith Exemplified in Antediluvian Times (Heb. 11:4–7)

Three pattern men are selected by the Holy Spirit from the dispensation of conscience, which extended from the expulsion of our first parents from Eden to the destruction of "the world that then was," by the flood. Eliphaz, in the book of Job, directs attention to "the way which wicked men of old have taken, whose foundation was overflown with a flood: which said unto God, Depart from us."

Here, on the other hand, we are asked to contemplate three men who found their delight in God, and glorified Him by faith in a day when corruption and violence were rapidly filling the earth.

In Abel we have the basic truth that approach to God is on the ground of sacrifice; and that the offering up of a living creature's blood was designed of God to illustrate the sacrifice and death of His own blessed Son. That it was not any mere assumption on the part of Abel that led him to select a lamb of the flock for his offering, nor simply an arbitrary act of his will is evident from the fact that we are told, "By faith Abel offered unto God a more excellent sacrifice than Cain." Faith is taking God at His word. Manifestly, therefore, we are to understand that God Himself had revealed the truth that approach to Him must be by sacrifice. This revelation Cain impudently ignored. Abel acted in accordance with God's revealed will, and in so doing, "obtained witness that he was righteous, God testifying of his gifts: and by it he being dead yet speaketh." His righteousness consisted in believing God and acting accordingly.

In Enoch we see a further truth illustrated. He walked with God by faith, and faith that triumphed over death. He was taken to heaven without dying. As in the case of Elijah afterward, men sought in vain for his body. He was not found because God had translated him. Before his rapture, he had the testimony that he pleased God. We may well be reminded of our Lord's words, "I am the resurrection, and the life: he that believeth in me, though he were dead, yet shall he live: and whosoever liveth and believeth in me shall never die" (John 11:25–26). Just as Enoch was translated before the judgment of the flood came, so those now who walk by faith and are living upon the earth at the return of our Lord Jesus to gather His own to Himself, will be caught up to meet Him in the air without passing through death.

Thus we see that Enoch's faith and ours are of the same character. We see that he was a regenerated man who was justified before God and walked with God in the power of faith. "Without faith, it is impossible to please Him." The natural man could not in any dispensation live to the glory of God, therefore the need of a second birth. For he that would draw nigh to God must have faith in Him, truly believing that He exists and that He will reward those who seek Him out. This is in full accord with the great declaration of Romans 2:6–8. No man in any dispensation honestly sought after God and failed to find Him, for He always revealed Himself to faith.

In Noah we have faith triumphing over judgment. Here again we are called to contemplate a man who in a dark and difficult day heard the voice of God in his inmost soul, and was oracularly warned of Him concerning something which, in the very nature of things, he could not see; but he believed God and, moved with fear, prepared an ark for the saving of his house. By acting thus upon the Word of the Lord, he condemned the world and became heir of the righteousness which is according to faith. The very building of the ark was in itself a sermon to the antediluvians. Every tap of Noah's hammer was a part of his preaching of righteousness to that generation. It declared him to be a man of faith, and it manifested their utter unbelief.

When God said to Noah, "Come thou and all thy house into the ark, for thee have I seen righteous in this generation," it was primarily the righteousness which is of faith of which He spoke. But where there is real faith in the soul, the life will correspond to that righteousness which is divinely imputed.

Faith in View of the Promised Seed (Heb. 11:8–16)

Noah belongs to two dispensations. His testimony closed that in which man had been tried and found wanting under conscience. As he stepped out of the ark and built his altar upon the new earth, another dispensation began, that of human government, and of promise and testimony, which we generally speak of as the patriarchal age. In this, Abraham becomes the distinctive figure, though God graciously gives a very large place to the faith of Sarai, his wife, and that in spite of the fact that the casual reader of the record in

Genesis might imagine that Sarai had very little faith indeed, when she had to be reproved by the angel for her unseemly laughter in the face of the divine declaration that she should have a son.

The very first step that Abraham took, as recorded in the Word, was one of faith. "By faith Abraham, being called to go out into a place which he should after receive for an inheritance, obeyed; and he went out, not knowing whither he went." There is no mention here of his failures—the stop in Haran, nor yet the fact that he did not immediately separate himself from his kindred, but that actually his father seems to have taken the initiative in this first step. But the faith that led to the entire movement was that of Abraham, to whom God had revealed Himself in Ur of the Chaldees. According to the statement of Joshua, there can be little doubt that Abraham's family was idolatrous. He said, "Your fathers dwelt on the other side of the flood in old time, Terah, the father of Abraham, and the father of Nachor: and they served other gods" (Josh. 24:2). But it was to a young man brought up in these circumstances that the living God revealed Himself, and from that moment faith sprang up in Abraham's soul. He was a new man, born of God, though he did not yet have the clear testimony that he was justified by faith. That came later with the fuller revelation of the promised Seed.

By faith he trod the pilgrim path, dwelling as a stranger in the land of promise, his tent and his altar witnessing to the double character of the pilgrim and the worshipper. Isaac and Jacob, the heirs with him of the same promise, followed his example. The tenth verse suggests that God had made wonderful revelations to Abraham, which are not recorded in the Old Testament, for we read, "He looked for a city which hath foundations, whose builder and maker is God." This city is never described for us until we come to the closing chapters of the book of Revelation. It is the home of all the saints of God, and toward that Abraham looked and, because of its glory, counted things then present as of small moment.

Sarai's faith, though obscured at times, shines out brightly indeed when we remember how utterly impossible from a human standpoint it was that she should ever become the mother of the promised child. That there was a breakdown on the part of both herself and her husband—a breakdown which brought Hagar into the home and led to unhappy circumstances later—is perfectly true, but all this was only temporary. That which God delights to remember of Sarai is that she "judged him faithful who had promised." And so the apostle reminds us, "There have been born of one, and that of one become dead, even as the stars of heaven in multitude, and as the countless sand which is by the sea shore" (DARBY).

So this particular section concludes with the declaration that all of these died in faith. They left this scene without having received all that was promised, but the promises became to them very real, and they laid hold of them, and because of these promises confessed themselves strangers and pilgrims on the earth. To relinquish present things in view of future blessing is to declare openly that one is seeking a country. No one can truly relinquish this world below until he has seen by faith a better and brighter world above. Had the patriarchs desired, they could have returned to the temporal things from which God had called them out, but they sought a better, that is, a heavenly country; they let go of present advantage as they reached out for that which God had promised. Therefore, it is His delight to own them now as His own, and to link His name with theirs for whom He has prepared a city. May it be ours to follow in their train, and thus as strangers and pilgrims press on to the rest that remains for the people of God. One is reminded of J. Denham Smith's beautiful words:

> Rise up and hasten,
> My soul, haste along!
> And speed on thy journey
> With hope and with song.
> Home, home is nearing,
> 'Tis coming into view,
> A little more of toiling,
> And then to earth adieu.

Why should we linger
  When Heaven lies before?
Earth's fast receding
  And soon will be no more;
Its joys and its treasures,
  Which once here we knew,
Now never more can charm us,
  With such a goal in view.

Faith Exemplified in the Patriarchs from Abraham to Joseph (Heb. 11:17–22)

Beginning with the seventeenth verse we have another distinct series bearing witness to the power of faith. Abraham is brought in again, but in an altogether different connection. Heretofore he has been before us as the expectant believer waiting upon God to fulfill His promise to give him a son. We have seen how that faith was rewarded in due time, after nature had been proved to be utterly powerless and as good as dead. Now we have the same patriarch manifesting faith under new and even more trying circumstances. The promised son had been given, but to the father's heart there came the demand from God to give that son back to Him, and to do it in such a way as to prefigure the sacrifice of God's own Son upon the cross, and in a manner that transcended every other Old Testament type. The scene in Genesis 22 is one that moves every regenerated soul to worship and praise as he reads it, presenting as it does the father and the son going to the place of sacrifice. Twice in that chapter we get the tender and meaningful words, "They went both of them together" (vv. 6, 8). How strikingly this sets forth that mystic journey of the Father and the Son from the throne of glory to the cross of Calvary. Of these divine persons it may also be said, "They went both of Them together." It tells us something of what it meant to God to give His Son to die on behalf of sinful man, as well as reminding us of what it meant to Jesus to take our place in judgment and die in our room and stead.

In Abraham's case, God, as F. W. Grant has well said, "spared that father's heart a pang which He would not spare His own." So Abraham offered up his son in figure only, and in figure received him again from the dead. We need not dwell on the shock that must have been his when the command first came to take his son and offer him as a burnt offering. If he did so, how could the words ever be fulfilled, "In Isaac shall thy seed be called"? But faith triumphed over an apparently insurmountable difficulty so far as nature was concerned, and Abraham bound his son upon the altar and actually took the knife to slay him, "accounting that God was able to raise him up, even from the dead." It was faith at its highest, triumphing over every question that the human mind could raise, and depending upon the living God who is the God of resurrection to work out His own wondrous purpose of grace. Such faith could not fail of reward.

The next character mentioned is Isaac himself, and singularly enough his quiet uneventful life is passed over, and it is in connection with the blessing pronounced upon Jacob and Esau concerning things to come that his faith shines out. Yet if we read the Old Testament record it would seem as though he had failed completely at that very point, and had only conferred upon Jacob the blessing of Abraham because his wife and younger son conspired together to deceive him. But the blessing once given, Isaac seems to have risen above his own feelings and preferences, and recognized that God had overruled, and so he later confirmed the blessing to Jacob while giving to Esau a lesser one, and in both he manifested his faith in the Abrahamic covenant. We might have thought that faith was at a very low ebb indeed in this instance, but beneath all Isaac's own confused predilections, God makes it evident that He discerned real faith in the manner in which he blessed his sons.

In Jacob's case too, it was when he was dying that faith shone out most triumphantly. After a checkered life of mingled self-will and subjection to God, during all of which he was under the divine discipline because of failure, he saw with clear unhindered vision the future of his people when, as he was about to leave this world, he blessed Ephraim and Manasseh, putting the younger before the firstborn in a manner that manifested the reality of his faith, as he worshipped, bowing upon the top of his staff. His had been a long life for self and a short life for God, but he passed off the scene as a worshipper, triumphing by faith.

It may seem a singular thing, when we think of the wonderful life of Joseph, a man in whom faith was markedly manifested throughout, that once more our attention is focused upon something that took place just before he died. But in his case it was clearly the culmination of his entire pilgrimage. Though he attained to great honor in Egypt, he ever realized that his home was not there, and he maintained his pilgrim character to the very last. Therefore, as he was about to die, he reminded the children of Israel that Canaan was their proper inheritance, and gave commandment that when they should leave Egypt to return to the land God had given to their fathers, they should carry with them his bones. This might seem a little thing, but God has drawn particular attention to it in several Scripture passages. It is in Genesis 50:25 that we have the commandment referred to. Then in Exodus 13:19 we are told how this commandment was obeyed when the hosts of Israel went out of Egypt. All through their wilderness wanderings they carried the bones of Joseph, typical surely for us of our present responsibility ever to "bear about in the body the dying of the Lord Jesus, that the life also of Jesus may be made manifest in us." Then in Joshua 24:32 we are told how the bones of Joseph were buried at last in that parcel of ground which Jacob bought of the sons of Hamor, the father of Shechem, there to rest until the morning of the first resurrection. It was toward this that Joseph's faith evidently looked expectantly, and this enabled him to maintain his alienage in Egypt, a type of this present evil world. And so this series ends, and in the next verse another begins.

Varied Experiences of Faith from Moses to the Later Prophets (Heb. 11:23–40)

It is Moses, the lawgiver, who occupies the largest place in this section, and in him we see faith working under varied circumstances.

Although Providence had placed him in Pharaoh's house and probably made him heir to the throne, his faith took him out of the palace and sent him into the wilderness. For when he had come to full age, after forty years learning the wisdom of the Egyptians, he refused to be called the son of Pharaoh's daughter and, recognizing his relationship with the nation of slaves, he fled from the Egyptians, and sought a home in the desert. From the people of Israel the Messiah was to come, and because of his faith in Him, Moses chose rather to "suffer affliction with the people of God, than to enjoy the pleasures of sin for a season." For him to go on in Pharaoh's court acquiescing in his designs against Israel, would indeed have been to purchase present ease and comfort at the expense of future judgment, for he saw that such a course was sinful in itself and its pleasures only for a season. The reproach of Christ meant more to him than Egypt's riches and honors, for he looked ahead to the coming day of reward. If it be asked in what sense he could be said to know anything of the reproach of Christ, the answer of course is that "Christ" is simply the Greek word that represents the Hebrew "Messiah." And so for Messiah's sake Moses forsook Egypt. By faith he gave up all his privileges there and, in spite of great trials, endured as seeing Him who is invisible. It is only faith that discerns the invisible God who transcends all circumstances. In the obedience of faith, Moses observed the Passover according to the commandment of the Lord, he and all Israel finding shelter from the judgment of the last great plague beneath the sprinkled blood. What a picture of that wondrous place of refuge which the believer now has, sheltered by the blood of Christ!

And as by faith they were redeemed by blood, so by the same faith in active exercise, they were redeemed by power as they went forward at God's command, passing through the Red Sea on dry land, which the Egyptians in vain attempted, only to be overthrown beneath the mighty waters. This twenty-ninth verse brings out very clearly the difference between faith and presumption. Moses and his people passed through the Red Sea by faith because they acted in obedience to the Word of God. The Egyptians had no such testimony, but they presumed that what Israel had done, they too could do, and learned too late their mistake.

Joshua, the new leader, led the people into the land where their first victory was another demonstration of the power of faith, as the walls of Jericho fell after being compassed about by the Israelite army for seven days. But the very catastrophe that brought judgment on the people of Jericho proved to be the means of the salvation of the harlot Rahab, whose faith triumphed over the most adverse circumstances, and gave her an interest in the God of Israel, and a place among His people, even to bringing her into the ancestral line of our Lord Jesus Christ.

Other Old Testament heroes there were, too numerous to mention, who exemplified the same mighty power of faith. Gideon, Barak, Samson, Jephthah, David, and Samuel are indicated by name, and it is a comfort to our own hearts to see some of these in this list, for we might have questioned whether real faith wrought in such as Samson, Jephthah, and even Barak, if we did not have this divine attestation to the reality of their link with God. The goodly company of the prophets, too, are on this honor roll. It moves the heart to its deepest depths to read, in verses 33–38, of what this world accorded those whom God delights to honor. Through faith they subdued the foes of God and man, wrought righteousness in a world of sin, and obtained divine promises because they claimed them in faith. Some stopped the mouths of lions, like Daniel and Samson; quenched the violence of fire, like the three Hebrew children; escaped the edge of the sword, as did Jehoshaphat; and many another one out of weakness was made strong, thus evidencing the fact that divine strength is perfected in human weakness. Men naturally cowardly or fainthearted became valiant warriors, turning to flight the armies of the stronger opponents of the people of God. On more than one occasion they received their dead children raised to life again, and others who seemed defeated here were yet to triumph after all, enduring cruel torture for the sake of the truth rather than accept deliverance coupled with compromise, knowing assuredly that they would be rewarded in the first resurrection. Others, we are told, were severely tested by mockings and scourgings, bonds and imprisonment; some were stoned, others sawed asunder, as tradition says was the fate of Isaiah. They were tempted in every conceivable manner; some were slain with a sword, or banished from their loved ones, obliged to wander about clothed only in sheepskins and goatskins, being destitute, afflicted, tormented, finding insecure dwellings in deserts, mountains and caves of the earth; but concerning them all, God Himself has written the precious epitaph, "Of whom the world was not worthy."

All of these were enabled to triumph by faith, which, as we have seen, is the conviction of things hoped for, and so they looked on to the future, not receiving in their own day the promise that God had assured them would yet be theirs. He, having foreseen in His divine counsels that the better things of the new dispensation would not come in until our day, left them to wait until after the death of Christ to come into fullness of blessing, "that they without us should not be made perfect."

This last expression is most suggestive, and in itself is clear evidence of the conscious existence of believers between death and resurrection. How could these Old Testament saints now be made perfect when they passed away without receiving the promise, if they were not conscious in the disembodied state? It is anticipating a little to draw attention to the twenty-third verse of chapter 12, but there we find the Holy Spirit insisting on this very truth. We as Christians have now come into unison with "the spirits of just men made perfect." Old Testament saints could not be made perfect as pertaining to the conscience until the finished work of Christ had settled the sin question, but the moment that the veil was rent, to them there came the same blessedness that is now the portion of all who believe the testimony that God has given. Such are perfected forever in His sight.

In other words, we may say of Old Testament saints that their souls were all safe in God's keeping; their eternal salvation was absolutely assured; but the work upon which all this rested had not yet taken place. They were, if we may so speak, saved on credit. In the cross their responsibility was discharged, and now they, with us, are made perfect.

CHAPTER 5

Life in Accordance with the Truth of the New Dispensation

Hebrews 12–13

Warning and Encouragement to Go On (Heb. 12:1–17)

As we enter upon the last division of the epistle, we note that as in almost all of the apostolic letters it has to do with the practical outcome which should result from the apprehension of the truth set forth in the chapters that have gone before. For these Hebrews of old who had confessed the name of the Lord, it had indeed a special application calling them outside the camp of Judaism, with which they had been identified all too long after acknowledging the Messiahship and Saviorhood of the Lord Jesus. Judgment was soon to fall upon Jerusalem and those who were linked with the temple service. The time had come to separate completely from a system which God no longer recognized because His own Son had been rejected and crucified. All was now but empty form which once had been divinely appointed to typify the person and work of Christ. To attempt to reform that system or to restore it to a place in the divine favor was vain. The only path for those who would be faithful to God was that of separation from it all, but separation to the rejected One.

Here then the apostle begins with the familiar "Let us" of grace, so different from the "Thou shalt" of law. He says,

> Wherefore seeing we also are compassed about with so great a cloud of witnesses, *let us* lay aside every weight, and the sin which doth so easily beset us, and *let us* run with patience the race that is set before us, looking unto Jesus the author and finisher of our faith; who for the joy that was set before him endured the cross, despising the shame, and is set down at the right hand of the throne of God. (Heb. 12:1–2)

In considering these verses, the question arises at once as to just what the Spirit of God means us to understand by the opening exhortation. The "great cloud of witnesses" refers, there can scarcely be any question, to the heroes of faith already listed for us in chapter 11, and with whom are included, of course, all who in every age have walked in the same path of dependence on God. Are we to think of all these as spectators in an amphitheater looking down upon those who were contestants in the arena below? It seems to me it is not so easy to decide this question as some have thought. Our English word *witness* can be used in two very distinct senses. It may mean to behold, or on the other hand, simply to bear testimony. It would seem as though the original word here used has distinctly the latter sense, so that those of whom we have read in chapter 11 are really testimony-bearers to the power of faith. On the other hand, the apostle clearly seems to indicate that there is a sense in which we are surrounded by a great cloud of spectators who apparently are looking down upon us, while themselves witnessing to the grandeur of a life of faith. But in any case, it is intended to be a message of encouragement to those who are still in the place of testing.

Such are exhorted to lay aside every weight and thus outdistance besetting sin. It is not some one particular sin, I take it, the same in all cases. But sin, as such, seeks to entangle each believer. The sin of unbelief is referred to particularly, no doubt, but this results in many forms of failure. There is no saint so holy but that he realizes he has certain tendencies, which if allowed to control him, would lead to the breakdown of his testimony. To escape besetting sin we are to lay aside every weight. A weight is not in itself a sin. It is simply a hindrance, something that impedes the racer. If we think of besetting sin as a savage beast, and the man of faith running his appointed race with this beast ever following hard after him, we can see at once the striking picture presented here. We who would outrun sin must not be loaded down with needless weights. Each knows for himself what these hindrances are. It is when they are cast aside that he is able to leave the fierce pursuer behind. But such an one must have an Object before him as well, in order to keep up his courage unto the end; and so the believer is bidden to look steadfastly upon Jesus, who Himself is the Leader and Completer of faith; not exactly "*our* faith," as we have it in the King James Version, but of faith as such. His was the life of faith in all its perfection. In view of the joy set before Him, the joy of having His own redeemed ones with Him in the glory, He went through the bitter anguish of the cross, despising its shame, and now, in answer to all that, God the Father has seated Him as Man at His own right hand on the eternal throne. His victory is ours as we recognize our union with Him.

He then is to be the Object before the souls of His people. And so we read, "Consider him that endured such contradiction of sinners against himself, lest ye be wearied and faint in your minds" (v. 3). In the hour of discouragement when one feels inclined to cry with Jacob, "All these things are against me," lift up your eyes, tempted one, and look upon Him who knew such grief as you shall never know, and yet who sits as Victor now in highest glory. Let Him be your heart's Object. Let Him be your soul's delight, and lifted above the cares and griefs of the present moment, you will be enabled to run your appointed race without becoming weary and without fainting.

And if at times you are tempted to think that no one else has ever been called upon to endure such trials as those to which you have been exposed, learn to think soberly in regard to this, for the fact of the matter is, many another has suffered unspeakable tortures, such as you have not known. "Ye have not yet resisted unto blood, striving against sin" (v. 4). It is not of Christ he speaks here, but of those who for Christ's sake loved not their lives unto death, but chose death rather than any compromise with iniquity. To this great and final test manifestly no living saint has yet been called.

Then, too, it is so easy to forget what is implied in the exhortation, "My son, despise not thou the chastening of the Lord, nor faint when thou art rebuked of him: for whom the Lord loveth he chasteneth, and scourgeth every son whom he receiveth." This is a quotation from Proverbs 3:11–12, and is confirmed in Job 5:17 and Psalm 94:12. It tells us that chastening is for our good.

Naught can come to us
But what His love allows.

Every sorrow the children of God are permitted to endure is designed by God for blessing. Chastening is not necessarily punishment. It is rather instruction by discipline. It is the divine method used for our education. Notice that there are three attitudes we may take toward the Lord's chastening. It is possible to despise it. He who does so but hardens himself against God and refuses to learn the lessons which the chastening is designed to teach him. "Who hath hardened himself against Him and prospered?" On

the other hand, one may faint under the chastening. There are shrinking timid souls who lose all courage when trouble comes. Like "Little-Faith" in *The Pilgrim's Progress*, they are constantly cast down by the trials of the way. This too is to miss the blessing. But the eleventh verse gives the third alternative, and to that we shall come in due time.

"If ye endure chastening," we are told, "God dealeth with you as with sons; for what son is he whom the father chasteneth not? But if ye be without chastisement, whereof all are partakers, then are ye bastards, and not sons." God disciplines His own children. He reserves the unjust unto the day of judgment to be punished. And in this way we may see the difference between a backsliding child of God and one who has never truly known the Lord, but has made a profession, and then turned back into the world. The first will ever be under the chastening hand of God, if going on in self-will. The latter may seem remarkably free from any evidence of the divine disfavor, but he only proclaims thereby the sad fact that he was never a regenerated person at all, but simply one who bore the name of son but had no rightful title to it.

As children in earthly families, we had fathers to correct us and we gave them reverence. Yet they were far from being infallible. They chastened us according to their own pleasure, that is, either as they thought best at the time, or because our behavior was such as to cause them discomfort. How much more ought we to revere Him who is the Father of spirits, who chastens only for our profit, ever desiring that we might be partakers of His holiness. He is never arbitrary in His dealings with us.

The trials to which we are exposed, in His infinite wisdom, do not for the moment give joy, but are often hard indeed to bear. "Nevertheless afterward" the chastening will yield "the peaceable fruit of righteousness unto them which are exercised thereby." This then is the third attitude we may have toward chastening. If we are exercised by it, and judge ourselves in the presence of God, we shall find rich fruit in our lives as a result, which will be to the praise and glory of God. And so the section concludes with the exhortation of verses 12–13: "Wherefore lift up the hands which hang down, and the feeble knees; and make straight paths for your feet, lest that which is lame be turned out of the way; but let it rather be healed." That is, let each believer walk carefully himself, considering those who are weaker, seeking to be rather an example than a hindrance, and endeavoring to recover any who have been ensnared and turned away from the path of faith.

There is perhaps no other truth along the lines of practical experience more salutary for us than that which these verses have emphasized. We are so likely to refer all our perplexities and difficulties merely to natural causes, and so fail to learn the lessons that they were designed to teach us by our ever patient God and Father. Or else we are likely to take everything of an adverse character as punishment, and thus become depressed in spirit because obsessed with the idea that we are constantly beaten with the rod on account of our failures. But neither view is a correct one. The truth lies in the golden mean. For the man of faith there should be no second causes. Everything will be taken as from the hand of God and even when one is called upon to share the afflictions through which the world in general is passing, the subject believer will recognize God's hand behind it all. But His hand is not necessarily lifted in punishment. It is the mind of God that, as a result of the very circumstances through which His people are called upon to pass, they shall learn their own feebleness and the untrustworthiness of their own hearts, and thus be cast wholly upon Himself, He who is our strength as well as our salvation and whose delight it is to manifest His Fatherly love and care to all who cleave to Him. We may be sure of this; when at last we stand in His presence we shall thank Him for every experience to which we have been subjected here on earth. We shall see how in all of these testing situations He was but making opportunities to display His wisdom and grace, but that in order to apprehend these aright, it was necessary that we should learn our own foolishness and the sinfulness of our hearts.

These lessons learned, what blessed fruit there will be in lives of purity and righteousness. And we learn by these experiences, as we go through them in fellowship with God, to enter sympathetically into those of our brethren, and so we become helpers of their faith rather than hindrances and stumbling blocks. No one can judge harshly of others, be unkind or unforgiving, who has learned his own unreliability and need of constant mercy, while walking the path of trial and testing under the discipline of the Lord.

In the four verses with which this section closes an exhortation is combined with a most solemn warning. In verse 14 we read, "Follow peace with all men, and holiness, without which no man shall see the Lord." It is important to observe that in this verse we do not have the positive statement which people so often substitute for what is actually written: "Without holiness no man shall see the Lord." This expression is capable of being utterly misconstrued and has tormented many an earnest soul who was seeking to do the very thing that the verse rightly read commands. The teaching has been based upon it that holiness is an experience called by some the second blessing, or the second work of grace, and that those who do not obtain this experience, although regenerate, will eventually lose their souls and will never see the Lord. But this is farfetched indeed and finds no countenance whatever in the text itself. In fact, the very opposite is true. We follow that which is ever before us. When we attain it we no longer follow it. And so here we are exhorted to follow two things, one manward and the other Godward.

First, we are to follow peace with all men. That is, we are to make that our object in our dealings with our fellowmen. Manifestly we shall never attain to this in the full sense. Even our blessed Lord Himself, though He came preaching peace, did not find all men ready to be at peace with Him. And the believer, however earnestly he pursues the ideal, will still find men who refuse to live peaceably. The second item is Godward. We are to follow holiness. This is to be the trend of our lives. We are ever to seek to become more and more like Him, the Holy One. Apart from this, no man, whatever his profession, shall see the Lord.

And so the verses that follow make it clear that if there be in the Christian company any man, who despite his profession, fails of the grace of God in not following peace with men and holiness toward God, he thereby gives evidence that he is still a profane person; that is, he is still in the gall of bitterness and the bond of iniquity. So we are bidden to take diligent heed lest this should be true of any of us and lest any root of bitterness should spring up through our means and thereby many be defiled.

The reference is to Deuteronomy 29:18 where God warned Israel of the danger to the whole congregation if any individual, family, or tribe among them fell into idolatry. Such would prove to be "a root that beareth gall and wormwood," bringing disaster upon the entire nation. "One sinner destroyeth much good" (Eccl. 9:18). For as we are told in the New Testament, "Evil communications corrupt good manners." Such an one was the fornicator of 1 Corinthians 5, and in the Old Testament we have a similar example in Esau who, in spite of all his privileges, was a profane person, who thought more of personal, physical gratification than of future spiritual blessing. And though the day came when he bitterly repented his folly and sought to persuade his father to reverse his judgment and give him the blessing he had formerly despised, yet he found no place of repentance in the mind of Isaac, though he wept before him and pleaded so earnestly. It is not, of course, that Esau himself could not have repented of his folly, though the special blessing was lost for good and all; but that once the blessing was given to Jacob there could be no change, "for the gifts and calling of God are without repentance." The warning is a most solemn one, for there were no doubt many in that day, and there are many still who mingle with the people of God, who yet have never judged the flesh in the light of the cross of Christ. Numbers of them will awaken to a sense of their folly when it is too late to obtain the blessing that once seemed so valueless.

Vivid Contrasts of the Two Dispensations (Heb. 12:18–24)

In verses 18–24 the Spirit of God places in vivid contrast the outstanding features of the two dispensations as connected with the old and new covenants. Two distinct circles are brought before us. In the first one are all those who still have their place on the ground of the Sinaitic Covenant, and hence are under the curse, as it is written, "Cursed is every one that continueth not in all things that are written in the book of the law to do them." In the second circle are found those who through grace have been brought into the blessing of the new covenant through faith in Christ and His finished work.

We read, "For ye are not come unto the mount that might be touched, and that burned with fire, nor unto blackness, and darkness, and tempest, and the sound of a trumpet, and the voice of words; which voice they that heard entreated that the word should not be spoken to them any more" (vv. 18–19). Could stronger language be used to show that no lasting blessing can come to fallen man through the law? The very circumstances under which that fiery law was given should have impressed upon him his utter inability to meet its requirements, and thus have led him to cast himself upon the matchless grace of God, which alone can undertake for a sinner whose fallen nature is in opposition to the divine will. But Israel, even though they shrank in terror from the manifestations of divine power, self-confidently declared, "All that the Lord hath spoken will we do, and be obedient," thus making themselves responsible to keep every commandment in order to enter into blessing. Yet we are told, "For they could not endure that which was commanded, And if so much as a beast touch the mountain, it shall be stoned, or thrust through with a dart: and so terrible was the sight, that Moses said, I exceedingly fear and quake" (vv. 20–21). If even the lower creation, made subject to vanity because of man's sin, would not be permitted to so much as touch the mount, and if Moses who might be considered the very best in all Israel, trembled at the thought of drawing nigh to God under such circumstances, what possible hope could there be of any ordinary man standing before Jehovah on the ground of legal righteousness?

But on the basis of the grace of the new covenant all those who believe in the Lord Jesus Christ have come into an altogether different sphere, a marvelous circle of blessing based entirely upon the precious shed blood of Him who was made a curse for us that He might deliver us from the curse of the law. Note the various items that are mentioned in the next three verses.

First, "Ye are come unto mount Zion." This speaks of God's free electing grace. We read in Psalm 78:68, "[He] chose . . . mount Zion which he loved." When there had been a complete breakdown under the former order, God exalted David, the man after His own heart, to the position of king in Israel, and confirmed the promises to him and to his seed after him, and established his throne upon mount Zion, which cannot be removed forever (Ps. 125:1). "Out of Zion, the perfection of beauty, God hath shined." From that sacred mount blessing goes forth to mankind, and eventually in the day of Jehovah's power, "the Lord shall roar out of Zion," "the law shall go forth from mount Zion," when "the Deliverer shall come to Zion" and all God's glorious promises be fulfilled, when "the Lord shall reign in mount Zion." It will be the center of new covenant blessing in that wondrous day. And for us at the present time, it speaks of pure grace superseding the legal covenant. It is not to mount Sinai then, the mount of law, but to Zion, the mount of grace, we have come.

Second, "Unto the city of the living God, the heavenly Jerusalem." This is not to be confounded with the earthly city of the great King, which will yet be the joy of the whole earth, for our portion is not to be in this world even when Christ Himself reigns, but we are to reign with Him from the heavenly Jerusalem above. This, of course, is the New Jerusalem, the bride, the Lamb's wife of Revelation 19 and 21. It embraces all the heavenly saints, that is, all those who have died in faith throughout the centuries, all who

in every dispensation believed God and were therefore quickened by His Spirit. The heavenly Jerusalem is preeminently the home of the church and therefore is designated as the bridal city; but saints of all other dispensations who have passed through death and entered into resurrection life will, as one has expressed it, be upon its "Burgess roll." This heavenly Jerusalem will be the throne seat of the entire universe of God.

Third, we have come "to an innumerable company of angels, a full gathering." The expression translated "general assembly" undoubtedly refers to this angelic company and not to that which follows, and is better rendered "a full gathering." We have come, in other words, into blessed association with the entire gathering of elect angels whose delight is to do the will of God, and who are themselves learning that will through His church.

Fourth, we are now made members of "the church of the firstborn, which are written in heaven." Firstborn here is in the plural in the original. The reference is not to Christ personally, but the entire church is called "the church of the firstborn ones," as distinguished from other saints to be called out and saved in a later day.

Fifth, "To God the Judge of all." There is now no separating veil, no cloud of darkness hiding His face; but in the blessed consciousness of justification from all things, we stand unabashed in His holy presence knowing that for us the sin question has been forever settled, and His perfect love has cast out all fear.

Sixth, "To the spirits of just men made perfect." These of course are the conscious spirits of saints of former dispensations. They are not sleeping, as some have imagined; all live unto Him. But until Christ's death and resurrection they could not be spoken of as perfect, inasmuch as redemption had not yet been accomplished. They were saved, we may say, on credit, God having forgiven them on the basis of the work yet to be accomplished by His blessed Son. That work now having been completed, they with us are perfected in the sense that they rejoice in the complete settlement of the sin question.

Seventh, "To Jesus the mediator of the new covenant." No fallible man this, such as Moses himself was, who because of his failure was debarred from entering the land of promise! Christ Jesus the Eternal Son of God, who became Man in order to take upon Himself our sin and blame, has met every claim of that violated law and now mediates the new covenant of free grace, into the blessing of which we have been brought.

Eighth, and lastly, we have come "to the blood of sprinkling, that speaketh better things than that of Abel." The blood of Abel, the first martyr, cried from the ground for vengeance, but,

> Jesus' blood, through earth and skies,
> Mercy, free, boundless mercy, cries.
> —Johann A. Rothe

He died not merely as a martyr at the hand of guilty man, but He offered Himself as an oblation upon the cross for our redemption. In instituting the Lord's Supper, the memorial of this redemption, we read, "He took the cup, saying, This cup is the new covenant in my blood, which is shed for many for the remission of sins." That precious blood speaks of His perfect spotless life poured out as a sacrifice on our behalf. In all the value then of His finished work, even the feeblest believer now stands before God and has come into this wonderful circle of blessing.

> And now we draw near to the throne of grace,
> For His blood and the Priest are there;
> And we joyfully seek God's holy face,
> With our censer of praise and prayer.
> The burning mount and the mystic veil,
> With our terrors and guilt, are gone;
> Our conscience has peace that can never fail,
> 'Tis the Lamb on high on the throne.
> —James G. Deck

Intensive Warning Lest the Present Truth Be Refused (Heb. 12:25–29)

Based upon this proclamation of new covenant blessing we have the solemn warning with which the chapter closes. We have already noticed that throughout the entire epistle, whenever any line of truth has been fully developed, a warning immediately follows concerning the danger of turning away from this revelation from heaven. So to these Hebrews, who were familiar with the claims of the Lord Jesus, but some of whom might not really have received Him in their hearts, the Spirit says, "See that ye refuse not him that speaketh. For if they escaped not who refused him that spake on earth, much more shall not we escape, if we turn away from him that speaketh from heaven" (v. 25). The greater the privilege, the greater the sin of rejecting the message. If God sternly judged those who refused the revelation given in the old covenant, what will be His indignation with those who refuse His present grace in Christ? Of old at Sinai, His voice shook the earth, but now He speaks of a time when He will shake not the earth only, but also heaven. He quotes from Haggai 2:6: "For thus saith the Lord of hosts; Yet once, it is a little while, and I will shake the heavens, and the earth, and the sea, and the dry land."

The apostle draws special attention to the opening expression showing that a shaking is in view which up to that time had not taken place. "And this word, Yet once more, signifieth the removing of those things that are shaken, as of things that are made, that those things which cannot be shaken may remain" (v. 27). May we not say that already that shaking has begun, and it will continue until all that man has gloried in will be broken to pieces, and he shall learn as Nebuchadnezzar of old that the Most High rules in the kingdom of men.

Already believers have entered in spirit into this, "Wherefore we receiving a kingdom which cannot be moved, let us have grace, whereby we may serve God acceptably with reverence and godly fear: for our God is a consuming fire" (vv. 28–29). It is not merely, as people often say, that God out of Christ is a consuming fire, or that He is a consuming fire to the unsaved alone, but it is His very nature that is in view. Consuming fire is holiness manifested in judgment, and God, who is light and love, must consume everything that is contrary to His holy will. For the believer, of course, this will mean eventually absolute conformity to Christ, when the last vestige of the flesh has been destroyed. Meantime we are to walk in grace, seeking to serve in newness of spirit and not in the oldness of the letter.

Sundry Exhortations (Heb. 13:1–6)

The doctrinal part of the epistle is now finished and the last chapter gives us, as is usual in Paul's writings, exhortations regarding the behavior of those who have laid hold in faith upon the truth heretofore declared. Brotherly love is emphasized. Those who have been drawn to Christ out of a world that rejects Him, should be characterized by love for each other. Alas, how often has it been otherwise!

Then there follows an exhortation to show hospitality to strangers, probably visiting servants of Christ first of all, and then of course others of God's children who might be in need of kindly entertainment as they pass from place to place, particularly those who were fleeing from persecution. Of old, some who thought they were thus showing courtesy merely to men, found it was their hallowed privilege to serve angelic visitors.

Many were already in bonds for Christ's sake. The saints were exhorted to remember them and to keep in mind all who were suffering, from whatever cause, as being themselves still in the body and therefore exposed to similar testings. None knew when his turn might come to endure affliction for the sake of that worthy Name.

In contradistinction to the loose and immoral ideas so common in that day, and even in our day unblushingly held by many, marriage was to be recognized as honorable because of a divinely ordained relationship, and to be preserved in purity, knowing for certain that those who violated the marriage covenant would have to face God regarding their sin.

The Christian too should live a quiet consistent life, not coveting what others might possess, but content with what God had given, knowing that in Christ Himself he had been granted more than any worldling ever knew. To have His promise, "I will never leave thee, nor forsake thee," was enough. What more could be desired until called Home to be forever with Himself. Therefore in faith, each believer could confidently exclaim, "The Lord is my helper, and I will not fear what man shall do unto me." Someone has well said, "God is a Substitute for everything, but nothing is a substitute for God."

> In that circle of God's favor,
>   Circle of the Father's love,
> All is rest, and rest forever,
>   All is perfectness above.
> Blessed, glorious word "forever"!
>   Yea, "forever" is the word,
> Nothing can the ransomed sever,
>   Nought divide them from the Lord.
>
> —J. Denham Smith

The Call to Absolute Separation from the Old System—Judaism (Heb. 13:7–21)

If we are correct in believing, in spite of what many have alleged to the contrary, that the apostle Paul was the author of this epistle, we can well understand how earnestly he would now plead for complete separation from the ancient system, the glory of which had departed since the rejection of God's Son. The dark clouds of judgment were hanging low over the land of Palestine. In a little while the sacred city would be a ruined heap. No more would the smoke of sacrifice ascend from Jewish altars. Moreover, most of the apostolic company had either been called Home or were laboring in distant lands. Paul himself was very shortly to be martyred by the executioner's axe.

With all these things pressing upon his soul, he urges the Hebrew believers to make a complete break with that system which had rejected the Lord of Glory.

And first he calls upon them to remember those who had been their guides in days gone by, who had instructed them in the Word of God, for here, in verse seven, it is evident that he has in mind those who are no longer with them. They are to remember their leaders of the past and to imitate their faith, considering the end, or issue, of their manner of life. These men for Christ's sake had suffered and toiled, gladly resigning all thought of worldly preferment that He might be glorified in their lives. The object of their faith was Jesus Christ, who is the same yesterday, today, and unto the ages to come; the unchanging Christ ever abiding amid changing scenes who is to be the Object of His people's hearts. It is important to remember that this does not imply that our Lord's administrations are always of the same character. "There are differences of administrations, but the same Lord." He does not act in the same way in every dispensation, but He Himself abides the same in person. If this were constantly kept in mind, Christians would not confuse things which God has clearly distinguished. For instance, it is often said by those who do not think clearly, that because the Lord healed all the sick who came to Him when He was here on earth, He will do the same today for all who seek His help, because "He is the same yesterday, today, and forever." Strange that they do not go farther, and insist that He will raise the dead and restore to them their loved ones now as He did three times when here on earth. Such confusion of mind would be avoided if the differences of administrations were clearly apprehended.

The next warning is against false teaching. From a very early day men arose in the Christian companies and particularly in Jewish assemblies, presenting new and perverse teaching, against which it was necessary to warn the disciples. Some of these laid great stress on Mosaic and rabbinic commandments concerning meats and ordinances which were connected with the temple service and had no proper place in the Christian economy. And so he writes, "Be not carried about with various and strange doctrines. For it is a good thing that the heart be established with grace; not with meats, which have not profited them that have been occupied therein."

And now in verses ten to fourteen we have the direct commandment to come outside the camp of Judaism in holy separation to the Lord Jesus Himself. We have an altar, he tells us, of which they who serve the tabernacle have no right to eat; that is, our altar and our service are all of a heavenly character. Since Christ has died there is no altar on earth; but in heaven, that of which the golden altar was a type, abides, where Christ makes intercession for us. To talk of any other altar, as is done in Romanism for instance, and some sects of Protestantism, is to deny the truth of the finished work of Christ.

> No blood, no altar now,
> The sacrifice is o'er;
> No flame nor smoke ascends on high,
> The Lamb is slain no more.
> —Horatius Bonar

In the time when the old Testament ritual was still recognized by God, the bodies of those beasts whose blood was brought into the sanctuary by the high priest for sin, when the sin offering was presented to God, were burned in a clean place outside the camp. In fulfillment of the type, "Jesus also, that he might sanctify the people with his own blood," that is, that He might set them apart to God in all the value of His atoning work, "suffered without the gate." He took the outside place there to bear the judgment that our sins deserved, and now we put our trust in Him, the rejected One, as our Savior, and confess Him as our Lord. In faithfulness to the call of God we are to be identified with Him in His rejection; so the apostle exhorts, "Let us go forth unto him."

To these Hebrews this would mean even more than to believers in a later day, who have never been attached as they were to a divinely ordained system which was afterward disowned by God. The deepest affections of their hearts, until they knew Christ, were twined about that system, but the apostle, speaking as a Jew to those who like himself had owned the Messiahship of Jesus, says, "Let us go forth therefore unto him without the camp, bearing his reproach. For here have we no continuing city, but we seek one to come." It was a tremendous challenge to these Hebrew Christians. It meant the breaking of the most tender of ties, and would necessarily lead to the gravest misunderstandings, but in no other way could they be faithful to the One whom the nation of the Jews had refused, but who had bought them with His blood. They must imitate their father Abraham, who left country and kindred because he sought a city which had foundations whose Builder and Maker is God.

I need hardly dwell on the fact that this expression, "Let us go forth unto Him without the camp," has been gravely abused and greatly misused by many who would make of it the ground for separation from Christians often as godly as themselves, on the pretence that if they do not see eye to eye with them they themselves constitute the camp. But it is separation from Judaism of which the apostle is speaking; and not, thank God, from Christendom, which however far it may have departed in some respects from New Testament truth, has not yet been disowned by God.

In saying this, I would not for a moment be understood as condoning what is admittedly evil and unholy, but I do not think it can be insisted upon too strongly that there is no ground in this Scripture for ecclesiastical pretension of any kind whatsoever. Ruin and failure are everywhere, and call for humble confession and self-judgment, not for pride of position.

We next have two verses that bring before us in a very precious way the sacrifice which believer-priests are now privileged to offer, for be it remembered, all Christians are now holy and royal priests. As holy priests we are to "offer the sacrifice of praise to God continually, that is, the fruit of our lips giving thanks to his name." God has said, "Whoso offereth praise glorifieth me." As holy priests, we enter into the sanctuary to present our worship and adoration to Him whom we now know as our God and Father. Then as royal priests we go out to man on God's behalf, and so we have the exhortation, "But to do good and to share what you have with others, forget not: for with such sacrifices God is well pleased" (author's translation). Our priesthood has both a Godward and a manward aspect, thus preserving that even balance which is so characteristic of the Word of God.

We have seen, in verse seven, how the writer called upon the saints to remember those who in days gone by had the rule over them. Now in verse seventeen he stresses obedience to those who now care for them in holy things. "Obey them that have the rule over you, and submit yourselves: for they watch for your souls, as they that must give account, that they may do it with joy, and not with grief; for that is unprofitable for you." True spiritual authority will be manifested by real shepherd-care of the people of God, and when the Head of the church gives the pastoral gift, it is for the blessing of all. To flaunt such a gift or to refuse recognition of it is to ignore and despise the Head Himself. On the other hand to confound the pastoral gift with the so-called clerical order is utterly unscriptural. No amount of training or ecclesiastical recognition can make a man a pastor. It is the Head of the church Himself who gives such a "gift" to His people.

In true Pauline fashion the writer begs for an interest in their prayers. How characteristic this was of Paul! He says, "Pray for us: for we trust we have a good conscience, in all things willing to live honestly. But I beseech you the rather to do this, that I may be restored to you the sooner." At the most, he realized that in all probability it would not be very long until he sealed his testimony with his blood, and yet if in answer to prayer he might be restored to service for a little time, he would value this, while being in all things subject to the will of God. Who can tell how much each servant of Christ is indebted to the prayers of God's hidden ones? To bear such up before Him is a wondrous ministry, the full fruit of which will only be manifested in that day when every secret thing will be revealed and each one will be rewarded according to his own service. Let none think that it is a little thing to pray. There is no higher ministry, no more important office, than that of the intercessor.

The beautiful benediction of verses twenty and twenty-one brings the epistle proper to a close. How often the words have been uttered through the centuries; how preciously they still come home to every believing heart! "Now the God of peace, that brought again from the dead our Lord Jesus, that great shepherd of the sheep, through the blood of the everlasting covenant, make you perfect in every good work to do his will, working in you that which is wellpleasing in his sight, through Jesus Christ; to whom be glory for ever and ever. Amen." How blessed the title, "The God of peace!" It is found elsewhere in the New Testament, as we know, and it tells of peace made by the blood of the cross, on the basis of which God is now speaking peace to all who trust His Son. Having raised from the dead Him who as the Good Shepherd offered Himself in behalf of the sheep and shed His blood for their redemption, thus sealing the everlasting covenant, God has now made that same Jesus to be both Lord and Christ. Exalted to the Father's right hand, He is now the Great Shepherd guiding His chosen flock through the wilderness of this world. Soon, as the apostle Peter tells us, He will return in glory as the Chief Shepherd (1 Peter 5:4), to whom all the under-shepherds must render their account. Meantime, by His Spirit, He is working in those for whom He once wrought so effectually on Calvary's cross. By this inward work He is sanctifying His people to Himself, daily making them more like their blessed Master, to whom all the glory of their salvation belongs both now and for eternity. And so the "Amen" closes the doctrinal and practical parts of the letter.

Concluding Salutations: Paul's Secret Mark (Heb. 13:22–25)

The concluding salutations need not occupy us long. In verse twenty-two he pleads with them to receive the word of exhortation, which will cut right across all their natural inclinations, but which he was pressed in the spirit to write, because of the circumstances in which they were found.

His companion Timothy who had apparently also been in prison, was now at liberty, and he hoped with Timothy to visit again the churches in which these Jewish believers were found, if it should be the will of the Lord. Then once more he mentions their guides, those who had oversight in spiritual things, sending to them a special salutation as well as to all the saints. This recognition of their leaders would come with good grace indeed from the apostle Paul, for there had been many who sought to bring about a breach between him and them. But he himself refuses to acknowledge anything of the kind, and he recognizes them in their God-given place as caring for the souls of the saints. The Italian brethren, doubtless Christians in Rome, and elsewhere, joined with him in this salutation.

He concludes the letter by putting upon it what we have seen to be his own secret mark, "Grace be with you all. Amen."

While specifically set apart by God as the apostle to the Gentiles, Paul never forgot that he himself was a Jew by nature. He knew all that it meant for his people to declare themselves followers of the Lord Jesus Christ. His heart yearned over them, and he was jealous with a holy jealousy lest they should come short of their full blessing by temporizing and clinging too long to forms and ceremonies, the legality and carnality of that which had now become a mere lifeless system since God's own Son had been crucified. He would have them enter into and enjoy in the fullest possible way that grace which was the very centre and epitome of his message both to Jew and Gentile.

As we review the history of Christendom we can see today how necessary was this cleavage. The heart of man readily falls in with forms and ceremonies. It is only those who are led of God who worship in Spirit and in truth. On every hand men are turning back to ritualistic forms and liturgical systems, seeking thus to make up for the increasing lack of true spirituality and devotedness to Christ. Unsaved men can "enjoy" a "religious service," but only the regenerate can worship by the Spirit of God.

NOTES

Introduction: Authorship, Scope, and Outline of the Epistle

1. See H. A. Ironside, *Romans and Galatians* (Grand Rapids: Kregel, 2006).
2. This outline corresponds very closely to that of F. W. Grant, ed. and trans., *Numerical Bible* (New York: Loizeaux, n.d.), to which the reader is referred for further help.

Chapter 1: The Glories of the Son of God

1. Commentary on Hebrews 1:3 in J. N. Darby's translation.

Chapter 2: The Glories and Humiliation of the Son of Man

1. F. W. Grant, ed. and trans., *Numerical Bible* (New York: Loizeaux, n.d.), 23.